Matt Stone

MBI

This edition first published in 2004 by MBI, an imprint of MBI Publishing Company, Galtier Plaza,Suite 200, 380 Jackson Street, St. Paul, MN 55101-3885 USA

MBI titles are also available at discounts in bulk quantity for industrial or sales-promotional use. For details write to Special Sales Manager at Motorbooks International Wholesalers & Distributors, Galtier Plaza, Suite 200, 380 Jackson Street, St. Paul, MN 55101-3885 USA.

ISBN 0-7603-1767-4

On the front cover: Dodge's maximum-strength sports car entered its second decade in production with a new design for 2003. While its proportions and detailing diffes greatly from that of the original 1992-2002 Viper, the mission is the same: to be the ultimate American sports car. With 500 horsepower and a top speed over 190 miles per hour, few would argue a legitimate claim to that title. *DaimlerChrysler*

On the frontispiece: It would be hard to imagine a face anymore menacing than this: Dodge's Viper GTS-R concept stole the show at Detroit in 2000—and at the same time gave us a sneak peak at what the next Viper would look like. *DaimlerChrysler*

On the title page: All of the Viper's key design elements come together in this 3/4 rear view, including the sports bar, sidepipes, and snake-like shape. Cutouts at the trailing edge of the front fenders are not only a styling cue, but are necessary to exhaust heat from the engine compartment. *DaimlerChrysler*

On the back cover: Vipers Three: From left, a iper GTS-R race car, the Viper RT/10 Roadster, and the Viper GTS Coupe on the high banks of Daytona. While the GTS-R has undergone substantial redevelopment for racing, its connection to the streetcars is both clear and legitimate. The Team ORECA Vipers ultimately claimed an overall victory at Daytona's 24 hour endurance race in 2000. *DaimlerChrysler*

About the author: Matt Stone is the executive editor of *Motor Trend* magazine and has authored five automotive history books with MBI Publishing Company. He is often heard on the syndicated *Motor Trend* Radio Network, and he is a Chief Class Judge at the Pebble Beach Concours d'Elegance and sits on the Meguiar's Car Collector of The Year panel. A California native, Stone resides in Glendale.

Edited by Christine Hunter
Designed by LeAnn Kuhlmann

Printed in China

CONTENTS

FOREWORD

In the late 1980s, a group of dedicated car enthusiasts dreamed of creating the Ultimate American Sports Car. Not long after—on January 4, 1989, at the North American International Auto Show in Detroit—a one-of-a-kind Dodge Viper RT/10 show car appeared before the public for the first time, with the goal of testing public reaction to the concept of a back-to-basics high-performance limited-production extreme sports car. The reaction was stunning, as "orders" began to flow in before the show was over. Little more than a year later, the decision was made: Viper was a "go." The dream was quickly evolving into reality.

Reality hit like a ton of bricks. Loud, wickedly fast, hair-raising, outrageous, and exhibiting an unmatched road presence, the Dodge Viper RT/10 Roadster was the Ultimate American Sports Car. Automotive enthusiasts flocked to it.

A few years later, in 1993, the Dodge Viper GTS Coupe was displayed at the North American Auto Show in Detroit and the Greater Los Angeles Auto Show, where enthusiasts' senses were exhilarated in only a slightly more refined manner. More than just adding a roof to the Roadster, over 90 percent of the Coupe was new, and it boasted more power and less weight. The goal was to cast the GTS in the mold of the world's premier Grand Touring cars—and cater to a broader customer base than the Roadster. The Viper GTS Coupe hit Dodge showrooms in 1996.

Viper enthusiast Matt Stone expertly conveyed Chapter One of the Dodge Viper legacy (the RT/10 Roadster) and most of Chapter Two (the GTS Coupe) in the first edition of *Viper*. In this, his latest edition, he wraps up the GTS story—with the Viper GTS-R's unprecedented string of international racing triumphs that included three FIA GT2 world championships, three class victories at Le Mans, and the overall win at the 2000 Rolex 24 at Daytona—before taking readers through the evolution of Chapter Three: the Dodge Viper SRT-10.

In January 2002 Performance Vehicle Operations—or PVO—was formed, combining Chrysler Group's specialty and performance vehicle production

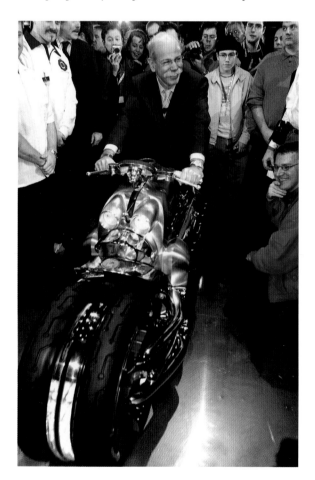

Dr. Dieter Zetsche president and CEO, Chrysler Group, aboard the Viper V10-powered Tomahawk concept at the 2003 Detroit auto show. *Chrysler*

engineering expertise with its motorsports and Mopar Performance Parts engineering know-how. Fittingly, the icon of the Dodge brand was PVO's first endeavor. Branded "SRT" for "Street and Racing Technology," the Viper SRT-10 brings Viper owners exactly what they were looking for: a true convertible with even more power, even lighter weight, and even better brakes, in a refined package that still exudes outrageous design and road presence. With its three 500s (500 horsepower and 525 ft-lb of torque from its 505 cubic inch V-10 engine), arguably the world's best brakes, and virtually unbeatable 0-100-0 mph times, there simply is no other car on the road like it.

And . . . there never will be.

Why? First, no vehicle has the history—or the ongoing ability to turn heads and drop jaws—that the icon of the Dodge brand does. Second, our vision at PVO is to continue to raise the bar, and to never rest on our laurels. And finally, our loyal Viper owners will continue to wave the flag of the car they love like no other owner group ever has or ever will. About 18,000 Vipers now cruise the world's roads and racetracks, and, remarkably, some 5,000 Viper owners are members of the Viper Club of America. They—and "a group of dedicated car enthusiasts" here at the Chrysler Group and PVO—will ensure that the Viper continues to retain its "Viperness," and remains true to our original mission: creating the Ultimate American Sports Car.

—Dr. Dieter Zetsche
President and CEO, Chrysler Group

ACKNOWLEDGMENTS

My sincere thanks first and foremost to the Viper's "Fourfathers": Bob Lutz, former Chrysler president and chief operating officer; Tom Gale, former Chrysler executive vice president of product design and international operations; Francois Castaing, former vice president of vehicle engineering and international operations and former general manager of powertrain operations; and the legendary Carroll Shelby, performance consultant to the Viper Project. Each has done well in their post-Viper careers: Bob Lutz has worked wonders in his capacity as Vice Chairman of General Motors of North America; Francois Castaing and Tom Gale have retired from Chrysler, though remain consultants to the company; and Carroll Shelby—at age 81—has just announced his re-association with Ford (expect new Shelby Mustangs and Cobras to follow). Special thanks to Mr. Gale, Mr. Lutz, and Mr. Shelby, who set time aside from their furious schedules to chat with me about the Viper, as did Roy Sjoberg, former executive engineer of the Viper Project; Ron Smith, former vice president of Dodge marketing; Pete Gladysz, former Team Viper chassis manager; John Fernandez, former Director of Performance Vehicle Operations and current head of the Chrysler Group's Motorsport programs; Dan Knott, Director of Performance Vehicle Operations; and the Viper's own "Grailkeeper", PVO Vehicle Synthesis Manager Herb Helbig.

A special thanks to Chrysler Group President Dieter Zetsche for contributing the Forward that opens this book. He, Chief Operating Officer Wolfgang Bernhard, Director of Design Trevor Creed, Dodge General Manager Darryl Jackson, and so many other Chrysler Group executives clearly committed to keeping the Viper not only alive and in production but at the top of the domestic performance heap.

Assembling the background information and archival artwork, arranging the shooting of new photography, and access to Viper cars for this project were all made possible by many current and former members of Chrysler's Public Relations staff, including Tom Kowaleski, Chrysler's former director of product PR, and Terri Houtman, manager of corporate image and brand PR. Major kudos to today's Viper PR guru, Todd Goyer, who helpfully provided a ton of information, made several interviews possible, did it all on short notice, and made it look easy. Others who helped along the way include Lisa Barrow, Lindsay Brooke, Juli Butkus, Dave Elshoff, Stephanie Harris, Jeff Leestma, Pamela Mahoney, Brian Zvible-

man, Art Ponter of the Chrysler Archives, and others who no doubt contributed behind the scenes. The copyrighted materials and trademarks contained herein are reprinted and used with permission from DaimlerChrysler Corporation.

Several of the profession's best photographers fixed their lenses on Vipers for this project: the incomparable John Lamm and racer/designer/ legend/friend Peter Brock, plus John Kiewicz, David Newhardt, Bill Delaney, and Wes Allison. I appreciate the editorial contributions made by writer types John Kiewicz, Steven Cole Smith, and Viperabilia whiz—and the Viper Club of America's first president—Maurice Liang. Our thanks as well to those folks whose cars were "snapped" along the way, but whose names are unknown to us.

Others who helped in one way or another: Rick Roso, marketing manager for Skip Barber Driving School; John Hennessey of Hennessey Motorsports; John Thompson, Mark Giannotta, Kim Vogt, and everyone at J.R. Thompson Company; Lee Corsack of Visual Graphics of New England; and Tom Lindamood and his crew at A&M Specialists West. Thanks again to Tim Parker, Peter Bodensteiner, Zack Miller, Christine Hunter, LeAnn Kuhlmann, and all the other professionals at Motorbooks International.

Deepest appreciation to my family and friends for putting up with all this car nonsense, which continues to be one of my great passions in life.

—*Matt Stone*

The Fourfathers' autographs grace the rear trunk panel of this RT/10. From Left: Carroll Shelby, Bob Lutz, Tom Gale, and Francois Castaing.

INTRODUCTION

The mere fact that the Viper exists today as a production vehicle is nothing short of amazing. Building cars is tough business these days: Society demands they be recyclable, biodegradable, nonpolluting, economical, safe-as-armor, and politically correct (whatever that means). Automakers need to satisfy a million government regulations and agencies, their own accountants and stockholders, and (somehow) the people who buy their product. This environment has helped create many supremely competent but hopelessly boring cars. Yet in the midst of this sea of seemingly red-tape-bound mediocrity, Dodge brought forth a 488-cubic-inch, two-seat roadster that will break most speed limits in any of its six gears. In the beginning, it had no door handles, roll-up windows, airbags, or air conditioning. Even though it has since acquired all these accoutrements, anyone who's driven a Viper knows it remains a visceral experience. Credit Chrysler Corporation's vision and guts in producing a vehicle designed and single-mindedly focused on performance, individuality, and driving pleasure—at a price tag not even approaching six figures.

The Viper served as the pilot within Chrysler for the cross-functional "team" approach to developing and producing cars, a philosophy that has proliferated throughout the company (and other auto makers) as a better way to get the job done. The significance of Team Viper cannot be overemphasized as a *major* element in the car's aura and success. Even though the players have changed over the years, and this group is now under the auspices of Chrysler's Performance Vehicle Operations group (PVO), the Viper still represents the company's performance flagship and Dodge's brand poster child.

Some of you may own or have read the previous edition of this book, first published by Motorbooks in 1996. The GTS concept had just been introduced, and we knew an updated RT/10 would come along with it for the 1997 model year. The GTS-R was beginning its assault on international sports car racing, and it was a pleasure watching it kick major butt all over the world, including back-to-back-to-back class wins at my favorite endurance race, the 24 Hours of Le Mans, in the years that followed. I knew it wouldn't be long before I'd be at work on an updated version of that original *Viper*, as there was little doubt in my mind that the car's story would continue, and that its popularity could only increase over time. The introduction of the new-for-'03 Viper SRT-10 was all the excuse we needed to give that original book a freshening, and a few more chapters.

I am not at this time a Viper owner, but I have put in many a mile at the wheel, and I have enjoyed them immensely. I also enjoy the infectious enthusiasm shared by Viper owners. Don't bother them with talk of the 1960s or any other era: For them, *these* are the Good Old Days. And even though the Viper is as masculine as a car can get, I'm pleasantly impressed with how many of them are owned, and truly driven, by women.

This is certainly not an all-encompassing volume on the Viper, as our space here is limited; future books will be written, and the car will continue to evolve. I hope you enjoy this look at the Viper's beginnings, its first 10 years as a production car, its impressive success on the world's racetracks, and the ripple effect it has had on other Chrysler products.

Thank you for purchasing *Viper*.

Author Matt Stone. *David Newhardt*

9

ONE

Viper Genesis

Chrysler might have been the last American company you would expect to set out and build an elemental, high-performance roadster such as the Viper. Both Ford and General Motors have an extensive history of producing high-performance sports cars. Ford has won Le Mans and has powered Indy 500 winners; Chevrolet has built what was (at the time) rightly called "America's only true sports car," the Corvette. But the smolderings at Chrysler were there and were probably first recognizable after World War II. At least two factors set the stage for its postwar performance awakening: the Hemi V-8 and chief stylist Virgil Exner.

History on display: VM02, foreground, and VM01 make a public appearance at the Pebble Beach introduction of the GTS-R racer at a 1995 press conference.

The fire power Hemi V-8, first introduced in 1951, gave Chrysler a modern, overhead-valve V-8 with exceptional performance potential; its basic architecture is still found in today's supercharged, nitro-burning NHRA top fuel and funny car drag racers, with outputs exceeding 6,000 horsepower. It was called "Hemi," owing to its hemispheric combustion chambers, which placed the spark plug in the center of the combustion chamber for more efficient burning and better performance. The engine grew to 392 cubic inches by the end of the 1950s. Virgil Exner, a talented and flamboyant stylist, came to Chrysler from Studebaker in 1950. He admired the design talent and coachbuilding ability of the Italian styling houses, or *carrozzeria*, particularly that of Ghia. Ghia had designed and constructed a number of styling exercises, or "idea cars," as they were often referred to at the time, for Chrysler. The cars had sporty flavor, and included the Plymouth Explorer, the Chrysler K-310 and C-200, the Chrysler Falcon, and a series of machines dubbed Firearrow. Several of these machines featured Hemi V-8 power. Though none made production per se, they had some influence on Chrysler design throughout the 1950s and into the early 1960s.

The Hemi's first real foray into a production sports car was not a Chrysler product but was a very American effort nonetheless at the hands of race

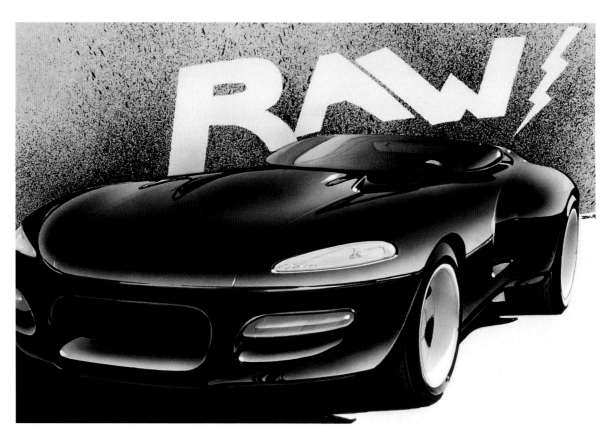

This styling concept drawing shows that the makings of the overall shape, rear sport bar, and hood-mounted exhaust vents were already in place in late 1988. *DaimlerChrysler*

No top, no side windows, no door handles, but Chrysler-powered and made in the USA: the Cunningham formula certainly provided inspiration for the Viper-to-be. This photograph was taken in August 1951, about 40 years prior to the first production Viper RT/10s.

driver, team owner, yachtsman, and car constructor Briggs Swift Cunningham. Cunningham had done reasonably well at the 1950 24 Hours of Le Mans endurance race in France with two Cadillac-powered entries; he once commented that "the French welcomed us to come back, but said to bring smaller cars." He began building his own Cunningham racers and limited-production street cars in Palm Beach, Florida, and turned to Chrysler's Hemi for power. Cunningham's racing creations were mostly taut roadsters, bodied by Italy's Vignale; they were truly the American Ferraris of their day. In the case of the C4-R, for example, the Hemi was tuned to deliver more than 300 horsepower, and C-4Rs were often clocked at well over 150 miles per hour.

Cunningham also produced handsome coupes and roadsters for the street, in an effort to help support

This early rendering testifies that many of the Viper's styling elements were cast early on, such as bulging rear fenders, low-cut windshield, hood vents, and an early idea for the RT/10s "sport bar." *DaimlerChrysler*

13

The shape is different from the final version, though note that one important cue is already in place: a V-10 engine. *DaimlerChrysler*

the racing venture. The first C-2s were constructed in 1952, and the final C-6 models in 1955, with most being Chrysler powered. Although Cunningham never did achieve his goal of building and driving the first American car to win Le Mans, he had racing successes at other venues. Cunningham would continue to compete successfully in Jaguars, OSCAs, Maseratis, and Corvettes. Still, when searching for the Viper's earliest roots, you need only look as far as, say, a Cunningham C-4R competition roadster, drifting through a corner, tires clawing for grip, Hemi V-8 barking all the way.

Throughout the 1960s, Chrysler performance went mostly in a straight line—and about a quarter mile at a time. Drag racing had matured considerably, the horsepower wars were raging between American manufacturers, and the muscle-car era was in bloom. A second-generation Hemi came from the factory packing four-barrel carburetors and 426 cubic inches. Other notable Mopar performance motors included the 413 and 426 Wedges and the 440 Six-Pack, running three two-barrel carbs. The nameplates these engines powered have all become significant pieces of

The Original Snake: Carroll Shelby

As one of the Fourfathers, Carroll Shelby played an integral and inspirational role in the Viper's development. The ancestral connection to the Shelby 427 Cobra comes through loud and clear. I spoke with Carroll in July 1995 to gain some insight on how this legendary race driver and car constructor feels about his relationship with Chrysler and about the Viper itself. Here are some excerpts:

Author: You are awaiting a heart transplant during the planning and development states of the Viper. Please describe your involvement with the car.

Carroll Shelby in 1993, at the introduction of the Viper GTS Coupe, which was inspired by Shelby's Daytona Cobra Coupe of the mid-1960s.

Shelby: I went to all the Viper meetings for about the first year and a half, and then it got so that I couldn't go anymore, waiting for a heart. All I ever did was keep preaching, "let's keep the weight down, keep the weight down," 'cause when you start building something like that inside of a big corporation, weight is always a problem.... My main input into the thing is that I sat down with Lutz and he said, "Let's build us a sport-car." He wanted to put the V-10 in it; I wanted to put the V-8 in it, and he won. The main contribution I made, besides the Cobra, you know, it being a modern Cobra, was working with Iacocca and meeting with him about every two weeks ... we were moving into a recession, and to keep him OK and writing checks every two weeks [for the Viper program]....

Author: Considering the environment in large automotive corporations, I think it's impressive the Viper ever got built.

Shelby: When people ask me about the Viper, when they say, "Oh, it has no roll-up windows," or when they're critical of the Viper, I say "If you knew what we had to go through, what Bob Lutz and I had to go through with Iacocca, just to get him to let us build it, then you [would] realize how badly we need to change the image of Chrysler, [and] you'd never say a critical word about it...."

Author: What about the Viper would you change?

Shelby: Oh, I'd whack 500 pounds off of it, but I'm not going to say that in a critical sort of way, because I don't think that if the corporation sat down and started to build the car again, with all the givens that they have, all they have to put in the car, I don't think they could save over 300 pounds....

Author: The Cobra had an approximate six-model-year production life. How long would you envision the Viper to be a viable, marketable piece?

Shelby: It's just according to how greedy they get! If they would build 250 cars a year, it would last for 15 years, but they aren't going to do that. They're going to saturate the market; the bean counters will take the place of common sense every time.

muscle-car history: Road Runner, Barracuda, 300, Super Bee, Charger, Challenger.

Beginning about 1973, big-inch performance went on hiatus at Chrysler—and everywhere else. Government safety and emissions regulations, unleaded fuel, the boondoggles that were called "gas crunches," and other factors all conspired to quiet the voice of factory performance machines. By the end of the decade, Chrysler had to contend with all of the above, plus crippling financial woes that nearly put it out of business. Then along came Lee Iacocca.

Iacocca was among the senior managers who contributed to Ford's success in the 1960s. After being fired by Henry Ford II, he took over the top spot at Chrysler in 1978 and was tagged as the man who could save the car maker from looming bankruptcy in the late 1970s. With tax concessions and a $1.5 billion loan guarantee from the U.S. government, a new management team, and some new products—including more fuel efficient cars, front-wheel-drive, and the modestly priced K-Car line—Chrysler turned itself around and stayed in business. It was also during

RENKERT 6-25-90

Shelby Cobra influences are clearly demonstrated in this mid-1990 rendering: wheel designs, paint scheme, and Daytona Cobra Coupe grille and headlight shapes. Team Viper also rendered this same concept in Ferrari red with wire wheels. Any wonder who their targets were? *DaimlerChrysler*

16

Iacocca's term as chairman that one of the Viper's key creators joined Chrysler: Robert A. Lutz.

Bob Lutz is a "car guy" of the first order, having been with General Motors, Opel, BMW, and Ford of Europe. He joined Chrysler in 1986 and in January 1991 was appointed president of Chrysler Corporation, which he held until 1998. You'll read much more about Mr. Lutz in later chapters.

Among the many things Bob Lutz, and more particularly Chrysler design chief Tom Gale, accomplished at Chrysler was to modernize and reinvigorate the notion of the "concept car" or dream machine as an instrument to let designers stretch their creative legs. They also helped a carmaker gauge potential customer interest and media reaction to a future design theme before committing to production. The Izod concept car of 1985 may even be seen as a link between the Cunninghams of the 1950s and the Vipers of the 1990s, since it was conceived as a front-engined, V-8 powered roadster. It never got beyond the mockup stage, however, and shows virtually no resemblance to the Viper in appearance.

Besides the Cunningham, the Viper's two most obvious progenitors would have to be the Corvette and Shelby's 427 cobra. The fiberglass Chevy two-seater had been making sales—and image—hay for GM for the better part of 40 years, a fact not lost on Chrysler management. While the 'Vette can be packaged for brute force or reasonable comfort, no such thing can be said of the Cobra: its performance ability and legend need no introduction here: Its brute force would prove to be a key to the design philosophy of the Viper.

When Bob Lutz assembled the Viper's Fourfathers, he chose a group of men— Carroll Shelby,

The final version of the RT/10 had taken shape in this late 1990 rendering. Very few details differ; this car has 5-spoke wheels, while the RT/10 was launched with 3-spokers, and the dual, external gas fillers didn't make the mix. *DaimlerChrysler*

Tom Gale, Francois Castaing, and himself—whom he felt had the skills and the mind-set required to deliver the Viper. The car had to be conceived, designed, engineered, built, and marketed in a unique fashion. For conceptual inspiration, he tapped on the shoulder of Carroll Shelby himself. What better way to ensure the Cobra vibe made it to Chrysler's no-nonsense roadster? The Shelby-Chrysler connection already existed, due to Carroll's role as a performance consultant to the company. The goal of Chrysler's design director Tom Gale was to create eye-searing looks and packaging. Bringing the Viper from the drawing board to the showroom required the drive of Chrysler's top engineering executive, Francois Castaing. Besides

being savvy businessmen, these individuals were all serious automobile enthusiasts. Shelby's racing success needs no further explanation, and Castaing was involved with Renault's Formula 1 engine program. Gale and Lutz each have a stable of performance-oriented machinery.

According to both Shelby and Gale, Bob Lutz was really the "spark plug" behind the Viper concept: build a modern-day Cobra using 1990s technology and design, with emphasis on performance above all else, yet make it producible by a large corporation and deliverable for a well-below-six-figure price. No technology-laden gimmicks were envisioned, not even ABS—just an elementally designed roadster with a

The Viper show car on display at the Detroit auto show in 1989. Crowd—and media—reaction was overwhelming, confirming what Chrysler was no doubt hoping to hear: the demand and the market was there. Though this original concept vehicle shares no body panels with a production Viper, it's little short of amazing that so much of the look made the translation from show car to customer's garage; often by the time a dazzling concept car sees production, its impact is watered down considerably. *DaimlerChrysler*

The interior of the show concept car shares no detail with the production version, though a considerable amount of the shape and flavor did carry over. This car carries a five-speed transmission.

huge naturally aspirated engine putting the power down to the rear wheels, a pure connection between machine, driver, and the road. Driving for the pure pleasure of it. As a marketing tool, such a machine could do wonders for Chrysler's performance image, which was flagging in 1988.

Based on little more than a few conversations in early 1997, Gale's Highland Park Advance Design staff began sketching the shape that would become the Viper. Even the earliest renderings put all the right cues in the mix: an open roadster form, long hood, short deck, arching fenders, and wheelwells over huge rolling stock. Windows? Door handles? A top? Forget 'em. This was to be a serious performance roadster. The Cobra cues may have been there, but the Viper was not then, and is not now, just a restyled or updated version of the Cobra.

The heart and soul of any such automobile is the engine. While it would have been understandable if the design team just spec'd out an updated version of the 426 Hemi, they ultimately found their power plant under the hood of an upcoming *pickup truck*. According to Francois Castaing, "One of the first major projects we got going was to put a new big V-10 on its way. Jokingly, we said 'That's the kind of engine that back in the sixties, [Giotto] Bizzarrini and [Alejandro] De Tomaso would have bought to create the great sports car of back then. You know, very powerful, torque, big gas American engine, put into a nice body.'"

Dodge's new 8.0-liter (488-ci) V-10 was to be an all-iron unit, too heavy for the roadster project, but if it could be cast in aluminum alloy and tuned for more horsepower . . . Shelby would later say that he initially favored the use of a large V-8, but according to commentary from the other three Fourfathers, it was "V-10 all the way."

When the major design elements were in place,

Roy H. Sjoberg,
Former Executive Engineer, Team Viper

"It's really the basic foundation: teamwork. The Viper was truly Chrysler's pilot for the cross-functional team. I believe the key to the Viper product is the Viper Team, not any one individual, other than our sponsor, Bob Lutz. It's been the team functioning together, coming to understand each other. Not always agreeing, and it's not always been happy times; there have been frustrating times. The evolution of that has brought what I believe is an excellent sports car, and an American sports car.

"There are five keys to good teamwork that Viper has.

"Number one is vision, and . . . Bob Lutz, Tom Gale, and Francois Castaing gave us that vision. Number two is product passion . . . everyone on the team has that product passion, and it can overcome a lot of roadblocks. Third is that it's a Team that's *hands-on*. Nobody steers the car from behind the desk. We are all hands-on, working on the product, understanding the product, from the craftsperson to the executive of the project, which is me. Fourth, which has been really key . . . is the empowerment and the acceptance of risk. In a large company, bureaucracy can overrun a small skunk works like we are. Management that empowers and accepts risk is paramount to success. Last is management by coaching. Those are the five keys to 'How did Chrysler do it?' and why the car is what it is."

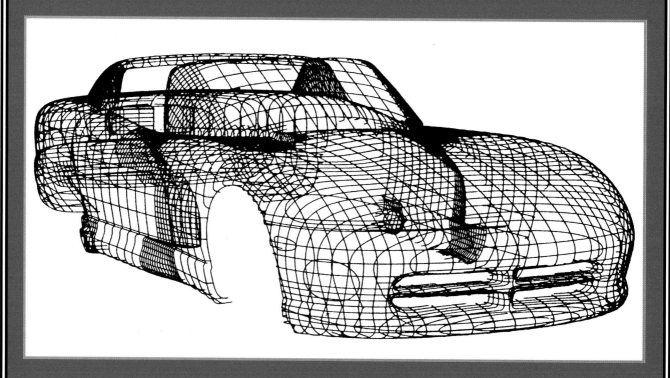

This CAD/CAM outline represents the shape of the original RT/10. *DaimlerChrysler*

Lutz authorized construction of show and test vehicles in May 1988, with an eye toward the 1989 auto-show circuit. When the brilliant-red Viper show prototype was debuted at the 1989 North American International Auto Show in Detroit, the Chrysler managers could not have anticipated the response. The car appeared in newspapers and in every enthusiast magazine. Mail, phone calls, and even deposit checks deluged the managers. It was immediately apparent that Chrysler had a potential hit on its hands, and had to at least study the factors involved in actually producing it.

Less than three months after the red roadster's Detroit appearance and a bit of discussion about hiring outside entities to build it, Chrysler announced the birth of Team Viper. This would be no everyday product, so there could be no ordinary way of

The interior of VM01 is business only, at best, as this vehicle's primary purpose was chassis and running-gear engineering.

Rear view of VM01 demonstrates lack of sports bar, so the high-mounted stoplight was affixed to the rear deck, as was the gas filler.

designing and building it. Castaing chose Roy H. Sjoberg, who had joined Chrysler in 1985 after more than 20 years with GM, to assemble the team that would transform the show concept to production reality.

Cross-functional teams are not new to the industry, but the Viper would be the first Chrysler project designed and produced in this format (see sidebar). Instead of passing the project from department to department, design, production, purchasing, and even suppliers would all be involved and empowered from the beginning. It was hoped this would result in less waste, less time spent, and a more unified vision of the final product. The concept has proven highly successful, and Chrysler and many other auto manufacturers have now developed products in this fashion.

Space limitations do not allow coverage of every aspect of the Viper's pre-production development, and more details about hardware and performance will come in Chapter 2. But suffice it to say that in May 1990, 15 months after that first auto show appearance, Chrysler announced that the Viper would be produced in limited quantity, with the first cars to be 1992 models. Viper was on the road to being on the road, so to speak.

And how did the car get its name? With the Cobra as its spiritual predecessor, a snake moniker was obvious. According to a quote from Bob Lutz in *Viper: Pure Performance by Dodge*, it came to him on an airplane trip. He toyed with the names Python and Sidewinder, but none had the right ring. "So 'Viper' seemed to be [the one]…it rolls off of the tongue easily."

So it does.

The interior of VM02 shows the wear and tear that comes from a hard life of engineering tests.

Left: The VM02 prototype. Much more of the Viper's final form is evident here than compared to the VM01.

TWO

On the Road 1992–1996

Clearly the Viper would be no ordinary vehicle, even among performance cars, so special development and construction methods, and a particular group of people, would be necessary to build it. Roy Sjoberg and other Chrysler managers interviewed hundreds of potential Team Viper members before selecting what they felt would be the most enthusiastic and qualified group. Its structure was much like that of a small entrepreneurial business, or perhaps a racing team, where problems are addressed immediately and solved quickly. An increased level of interaction would occur between management and the people who actually assembled the product.

An imposing sight in anyone's rear view mirror, the Viper crossbar grille theme has now been translated throughout Dodge's product line, even to the Ram trucks and vans; a successful effort on Dodge's part to unify the appearance of its product line-up and enjoy a bit of the performance-image rubbed off from the Viper. *DaimlerChrysler*

This cutaway of a 1992 Viper RT/10 shows the car's modern design and complexity. *David Kimball, courtesy DaimlerChrysler*

Each craftsperson would have a much higher level of responsibility for a car's assembly than in the past. They would often be involved in the build-up and installation of entire systems, rather than just attaching one component to each car as it rolled down a fast moving assembly line. Unlike many production-line environments, Team Viper would have direct communication with the designers and engineers, so process improvement could be effected quickly. Using a "custom-built" approach, groups of approximately five people would assemble one Viper at a time.

Chrysler selected its New Mack Avenue assembly plant in Detroit to be the home of Viper production. Beginning in 1990, the plant was remodeled into a modern facility, yet one that would not be focused on high-speed car production, but rather hand assembly and the craftsmanship required to build low-production, niche-market vehicles.

No multiple camshafts, four valves per cylinder, or other "exotica" for the Viper powerplant, just conventional V-8 technology brought up to modern standards . . . with two more cylinders, of course. *David Kimball, courtesy DaimlerChrysler*

Bob Lutz,
Former President, Chrysler Corporation

Bob Lutz is a rabid automotive enthusiast who just happens to be the president and chief operating officer of Chrysler. He spent time with BMW and Ford of Europe prior to joining the company in 1986. Among his other passions are aircraft, motorcycles, and fine cigars! Bob is a Viper owner and spoke candidly about what the car means to the company and customers.

Author: Chrysler has proven its ability to address enthusiast-market niches with Viper and concepts such as Prowler. How do you see Viper's success spilling over to other niches in the marketplace?

Lutz: Obviously, Viper has sent a strong signal [within] the corporation that it is a good thing to go with strong hunches, and if you have a clear vision on something that a small group of enthusiasts within the company would gladly and eagerly build for themselves, then you know that unless you're on a completely different planet, you know that if you do that vehicle, you're going to find a few thousand like-minded people per year [to purchase them]. That's really the philosophy that the Viper is all about, which is, dare to do something really terrific; not only despite the fact that nobody has tried it before, but because of the fact that nobody has tried it before.

Author: The GTS-R says a lot about Chrysler's enthusiasm for performance. In addition to producing the customer cars, do you envision a "works" GTS-R?

Lutz: None yet.... It's not currently planned, but I wouldn't categorically say we would never do it.

Author: How different will the Viper of say, 2001 or 2005, be from today's?

Lutz: It will be evolutionary. The car will get better and better. By the 2001 it will be highly likely that the shape will not be changed at all, but we'll unquestionably go for ever more performance enhancements. We want to keep it the ultimate affordable sports car.

Author: What would you change?

Lutz: I don't think I would change anything.... I suppose if we could wave the magic wand—and were not dealing with such onerous noise restrictions, which pretty much dictate what you do about exhaust sound—we are always enthralled with the way they sound when we use low-restriction mufflers ... you wish you had more sound and better sound, but it's hard to get there working around the ever-more-severe noise restrictions.

Bob Lutz with the Viper GTS Coupe he drove to pace the 1996 Indianapolis 500.

Like the Model T, the Viper was initially offered in only one color combination: red with gray/black interior. More colors would soon follow. *DaimlerChrysler*

The development of mainstream products often involves dozens, or even hundreds, of engineering mockups, prototypes, chassis "mules," and test vehicles. Team Viper, operating on both a strict budget and fairly short time constraints, did the job with only a few. Besides the original show vehicle, there were only a handful of engineering prototypes, plus a minimum of pre-production pilot vehicles.

The first prototype, chassis number VM01, was completed in December 1989 at a shop facility borrowed ("commandeered" would probably be a more accurate term) from Jeep. After the takeover, the shop became lovingly known as the Snake Pit. Painted white, the prototype carried hand laid-up fiberglass panels that were pinned to the frame; the rear "sport bar" was not yet present. Visually, VM01 resembled the ultimate production Viper only in terms of overall shape and proportion. For power, it

used a hopped-up Chrysler 360 V-8 and a German-made Getrag six-speed transmission.

The second prototype, chassis number VM02, was completed in April 1990. Painted red, this was the first Viper test mule to carry a V-10 engine, though it was an all-cast-iron unit, rated at 380 horsepower. A Borg-Warner six-speed transmission replaced the Getrag unit, and a good deal of the Viper's production development was done on this vehicle. It had side exhaust, a windshield, and an interior that were a step closer to what the production Viper would carry. Still hand-built of fiberglass, it was also tested heavily by the media, as it appeared in many magazine articles.

The original steel-bodied show car was also a steel-bodied prototype built outside of Team Viper's Snake Pit, by Metalcrafters in Southern California. Metalcrafters was a European-style *carrozzeria* that had developed numerous special projects and concept cars for Chrysler and other manufacturers.

The Viper's design and construction methods are a unique blend of time-tested, traditional elements, combined with modern componentry and materials. The philosophy was tightly focused on a brute of a roadster, but everyone at Chrysler knew they would be heavily criticized if they ended up with a throwback car or anything that could be written off as merely a factory-built "kit car."

Team Viper engineers chose tubular steel as the base material for the chassis. The steel space frame included a center spine structure with tubular outriggers to support the body panels. This method of construction was selected over a unitized, monocoque chassis for two reasons: it had a shorter development time than the more complex stamped-steel, stressed-panel design, and monocoque designs rely on the roof structure to stiffen the overall chassis—but the Viper had no roof. The required structural rigidity was easier to obtain using a more conventional frame. In the end, the Viper's chassis stiffness was exceptional for an open car, at approximately 5,000 pounds per degree of twist.

The suspension was fully independent, with unequal-length upper and lower control arms at each corner. With the exception of the front upper control arms, these pieces were fabricated from tubular steel. Two stabilizing toe links were used with the rear lower control arms, and gas-charged Koni coil-over shock/spring units with front and rear anti-roll bars summarized the underpinnings. A car that was designed to hit well over 160 miles per hour needs powerful, fade resistant brakes, and the Viper had them: 13-inch ventilated discs with Brembo calipers at all four corners. ABS? Never was a part of the mix.

A unique three-spoke wheel design would carry Viper through its first four model years. Cast in aluminum alloy, the wheels measured 17x10 inches in front and 17x13 inches in the rear. Michelin developed special XGTZ uni-directional radials just for the Viper, size P275/40ZR17 and P335/35ZR17,

Although the Viper's V-10 shares its displacement and basic architecture with the 300-horsepower, iron-block engine used in Ram trucks, it's really an altogether different piece. Lamborghini, owned by Chrysler and competing as a Formula One engine supplier at the time, consulted with Team Viper on the V-10's design and metallurgy. *DaimlerChrysler*

respectively—the same steamroller-like sizes found on the $250,000 Lamborghini Diablo. The rolling stock was controlled via power-assisted rack-and-pinion steering designed to provide maximum driver feedback and road feel, yet the car was easy to maneuver at very low speeds.

As mentioned, Team Viper had to get the car to production quickly, and on budget. This all but ruled out full steel body panels. Instead, a body and interior structure of several different resin transfer molding (RTM) composites was employed. Only the floorpan enclosure was formed of molded sheet steel. Besides the cost and time savings, the RTM panels yielded weight savings. "There's roughly about one-third weight reduction of sheet metal," according to Roy Sjoberg.

In the RTM process, glass fibers are placed inside a mold, the mold is closed, and resin is then injected to mix with the fiberglass, forming a finished panel. According to Russell Spencer, Viper technology development executive, "We...control the panel-forming process so precisely that when each piece comes out of the mold, it will require only 10 to 15 minutes of hand finishing before reaching a 'Class A' level appearance." This construction method also aided the ease of future appearance updates.

What could be a more important part of a performance sports car than its engine? Chrysler decided on a mix of pure big-block tradition and modern technology. Though there must have been some temptation to power the Viper with a modern-day rendition of the 426 Hemi or 440 Six Pack, in truth the car was virtually destined for the V-10

from the beginning. The earliest designs were built around it, and it is one of the features that gives the Viper its own identity, rather than simply copying the Cobra or Cunningham.

As mentioned earlier, the basis for the 8.0-liter "Copperhead" V-10 was the power plant being developed for the new 1994 Dodge trucks. But the truck engine's power characteristics would be all wrong for a sports car and the all-iron construction too heavy. "I guess you could say we took a straight-forward approach in developing this engine," recalls Jim Royer, Team Viper engine manager. "We didn't want to risk getting into exotic technology in so short a span . . . of development time."

Team Viper tapped the expertise of Lamborghini Engineering, which certainly had experience with high-performance street engines and would later

Original spec RT/10 interior spared the details, including air bags, and even air conditioning in the first 200 cars. *DaimlerChrysler*

Performance Comparison
Source: *Car and Driver*, July 1995

Model	0-60 (sec)	0-100 (sec)	1/4-Mile (ET@speed)	Top Speed (mph)	Price (as tested)
Viper RT/10	4.3	10.5	12.8 @ 109	168	$61,975
Ferrari F355	4.5	10.9	13.0 @ 110	179	$128,800
Acura NSX-T	5.2	13.0	13.8 @ 103	162	$86,642
Lotus Esprit S4S	4.4	10.9	13.0 @ 108	162	$87,904
Porsche 911 Turbo	3.7	9.4	12.3 @ 114	175	$106,465

Black-on-white gauges add a bit of a retro touch. Instrument visibility is excellent overall, as is performance from the heating and air conditioning system. Though it may seem a bit odd, one of the most pleasurable Viper driving modes is on a hot day with no top . . . and the A/C on full blast. *DaimlerChrysler*

develop V-10 engines for use in Formula One racing, although those engines were completely different units from those that would end in the Viper. It probably also helped that Lamborghini was a Chrysler-owned concern at the time.

The first goal was to reduce the engine's weight by at least 100 pounds. This was accomplished by casting both block and heads in aluminum. In keep-ing with the muscle car tradition, the V-10 would retain its overhead-valve configuration, with a single block-mounted camshaft. The block, with six crankshaft main bearings, employed an interesting cooling strategy. An external water manifold run-ning along the side of the block provided coolant to individual cylinders, which then flowed into the heads and back to the radiator. In the best race-car

31

All four colors available in 1995 take a bow; it's difficult to tell, but the second Viper from left is the dark green one, with a black car just to its right.

tradition, the alloy cylinders contained iron liners and forged alloy pistons; compression was a relatively low 9.0:1.

Though dual Carter AFB four-barrel carbs would not seem out of place atop the Viper engine, it's hard to beat modern hardware when it comes to intake systems and engine management. An aluminum ram-tuned manifold system with dual plenums works in concert with multipoint fuel injection to deliver a docile idle and the low emission numbers that the old Hemi could only dream of. Thin-wall, cast exhaust manifolds each expel the spent gases via a one-piece stainless-steel catalytic converter/muffler combination housed in what may be one of the Viper's most interesting performance statements: dual rocker-panel sidepipes, replete with labels warning "Hot Exhaust Pipe Below Door Opening" on the door sills. A fully electronic, distributorless ignition system works as part of a sophisticated engine-management computer system for maximum efficiency.

Every capacity of the Viper V-10 was "super-sized": At 488 cubic inches, it had the largest

mainstream production performance power plant in the world. Its official power rating (through 1995) was an even 400 horsepower at 4,600 rpm, with 450 ft-lb of torque at 3,600 rpm. (And the Viper's power output would climb steadily over the years.) Oil capacity? Not 5 quarts . . . how 'bout 11! Nearly 4 gallons of coolant! The 6,000-rpm redline may sound conservative when compared to high-winding Ferrari and Porsche power plants, but it's plenty high for an engine this large, and with so much torque on tap, more revs would serve little purpose. As a friend of mine, who is a big-block engine fanatic to an extreme, said of the Viper V-10: "Now that's a *motor*."

Backing the husky power plant was a Borg-Warn-er Model T-56 six-speed manual transmission, simply one of the best manual transmissions available. Its quick shifting action and capable synchromesh complemented the engine perfectly. The transmission case was also cast in aluminum and connected to the V-10 via a 12-inch single-dry-disc clutch. The 3.07:1 final drive incorporated a limited-slip differential.

The cockpit was quite traditional, focusing on driver input and performance: luxury seekers should look elsewhere. Comfortable, well-bolstered leather seats were separated by a fairly wide console. As the driver gripped the three-spoke, leather-wrapped steering wheel, the speedometer/odometer, tachometer, and warning-light cluster were in plain

The Viper logo pops up everywhere. Here it's embossed on the hood liner—in a *big* way. *David Newhardt*

view. Ancillary gauges (oil pressure, voltage, coolant temp, and fuel level) were in a binnacle at the top of the console, which also housed the Chrysler/Alpine sound system and heating, ventilation, and air conditioning (HVAC) controls. A security system was standard.

If anything spoke to the Viper's true purpose, yet seemed to draw criticism, it was the first roadster's weather protection system . . . or lack of same. Roll-up windows? None. Exterior handles? *Nada.* Hardtop? Zip. In their place, Chrysler designed a cloth top with zip-in side-curtain windows that did enclose the car but had to be considered vestigial at best. They're not particularly handsome and made the Viper feel a bit claustrophobic inside. When stowed, these pieces ate up a majority of the none-too-commodious trunk space. But hey, if you wanted to drive in a cocoon, you're looking at the wrong car.

The press, and the buying public, went bonkers for the Viper. Dodge had generated an overwhelming amount of PR, brand identity, and showroom traffic with the car. Every major automotive magazine had a Viper on its cover; some several times in the same year! Even today, a Viper on the road turns heads; one parked at the side of the road instantaneously draws a crowd.

It's also interesting that this most American of roadsters would be sold abroad. Export Vipers (branded as Chryslers, not Dodges) have metric gauges, revised lighting systems, tow hooks, wider license-plate brackets, an exhaust system that exits out the back of the car through the large dual pipes, and numerous other changes required by the varying regulations of European countries. One thing did not change: Vipers were as much of a hit in Paris or Frankfurt as they were in Los Angles or Cleveland, and they continue to be so.

It would be impossible to summarize the considerable media reaction, but a sampling of the commentary is worth note. *Car and Driver*'s Kevin Smith wrote, "Viper is one of the most exciting rides since Ben Hur discovered the chariot . . . It's intended to go fast, stop hard, hang onto corners, and give everyone in sight—driver, passenger, and bystanders—a thrill that will make their day." I particularly enjoyed *Sports Car International* editor Jay Lamm's thoughts: "The Viper is about having fun, playing games, and reliving a great childhood—maybe even somebody else's—and it's almost cheap enough for people to believe they could have one themselves someday, given a lot of hard work or a little good luck, it's an inclusionary sort of dream machine."

Ron Sessions of *Road & Track* reveled in his first Viper driving experience: "A driving route that included freeway cruising, delicious cut-and-thrust twisty bits, wicked mountain switchbacks, wide-open stretches of high desert, and some apex clipping hot laps at Willow Springs Raceway has afforded me a full measure of quality man-meets-machines bonding time. And with a tangled nest of split ends that passes for hair, I have the Viper-do to prove it." It would be hard to gather the impact of Viper's first four model years into one short paragraph, but *Motor Trend* came close when it said, "Nothing you can drive packs the personality, makes the statement, or snaps your neck like the Dodge Viper RT/10. Nothing at all."

Team Viper did not wait for model-year changeover to imbue the car with the latest improved hardware. Though collectors and historians, who track every little part change, may be driven a bit batty, the buyer gets the benefit of having the most improved version available at the time. Still, the 1992–1995 RT/10s stood quite markedly as the first-generation Viper. Beginning in 1996, the pace picked up considerably, with an updated RT/10, production of the GTS coupe, and the announcement of the GTS-R factory racer. The chronology is a bit interwoven; the initial GTS Coupe development began in 1992, the same year the RT/10 entered series production.

A Viper Coupe, called GTS

As surely as cars like the Cunningham and 427 Cobra were the spiritual predecessors of the Viper RT/10, progenitors of the same eras—such as the Ferrari 250 GTO, the Shelby Daytona Cobra Coupe, and of course coupe versions of the Chrysler-powered Cunningham racers—appear to have inspired the Viper GTS Coupe.

The first GTS Coupes were shown at the North American Auto Show in Detroit and the Greater Los Angeles Auto Show in January 1993. Though billed as "An Automotive Concept" at the time, the car was clearly designed with production intent, and crowd reaction was much the same as it had been to the original Viper show car just a few years before: Build it!

Shown in an arresting shade of metallic blue, sporting an exceptionally handsome chrome five-spoke alloy wheel design, and race-inspired white "Cunningham stripes" down the middle of the hood, top, and deck, the GTS looked for all the world to be an updated, streetable version of the aforementioned Daytona Cobra Coupe or Cunningham C4R-K. Only six Daytonas were built, all race cars, and they carried the Shelby team to the World Championship for Makes title in 1965.

I was with Peter Brock, Shelby American team member and designer of the Daytona Coupe, when the GTS was first unveiled at that 1993 LA auto show. Brock commented, "Tom Gale came to me with some of the original drawings of the GTS Coupe the previous August at the Pebble Beach Concours d'Elegance and asked my opinion of the new car. He wanted to make sure that I had no problem with the resemblance to the Daytona, especially the blue and white paint scheme. I was flattered that they would even consider asking my permission . . . Overall, it just pointed out what a class act Tom Gale was running with the Viper program."

Prototype GTS Coupes made the rounds among the automotive enthusiast magazines, and in 1994 Chrysler made the announcement that the Viper GTS Coupe would become a production reality for the middle of the 1996 model year (see Chapter 3). But making the GTS production-ready would take more work than just creating new fastback bodywork, so its development was done in concert with a substantially updated roadster.

Part of the tooling-up process for the Coupe would involve a new home for all Viper production. In April 1995, Chrysler announced that its New Mack Avenue assembly plant would be remodeled for the production of a new generation of truck engine. By midyear, a 345,000-square foot facility on Conner Avenue in Detroit had been acquired and established as the new Viper production facility for 1996 models and beyond.

RT/10 for 1996

The 1996 roadster is a unique piece of Viper history, a bridge between the 1992-to-1995 cars and the 1997-and-beyond models. This scenario is somewhat reminiscent of the 1968 Jaguar "Series 1 1/2" E-Type, which shared componentry with the multiyear run of cars before and after it. Because of the plant move and the completion of GTS Coupe tooling, Dodge only made plans to produce about 600 to 700 1996 RT/10s.

Immediately noticeable was the switch from rocker-mounted sidepipes to a rear-exit exhaust system, with two large chrome pipes just below the license plate. This was seen on the first GTS concept car, and was very similar to the system on European-delivery Vipers. The exhaust pipes still followed along

Dodge got racy in terms of color combinations for the 1996 "transition year" Vipers. They added contrasting stripes, and for the first time, offered wheels painted in colors other than silver. Note the new 5-spoke wheel design, shared with the GTS Coupe. Was the yellow and red "Mustard and Ketchup" paint scheme a jab at Ferrari, who used the same color combo on race cars in the 1960s? *DaimlerChrysler*

the sills, but now turned inboard forward of the rear wheels. The pipes then passed over the rear suspension and entered a tandem muffler. Some felt that the "five-per-side" exhaust sound of the original pipes left something to be desired; to this writer's ears, the new system was a vast improvement, even though they gave up a bit of the sidepipes' charm.

Three 1996-only color schemes were introduced; no more emerald green or yellow Vipers. The choices were black exterior with silver accents and a black interior, white with blue accents (more Shelby cues), or a combination quickly nicknamed "ketchup and mustard": red with bright yellow wheels and a yellow Viper logo just ahead of the front doors. Squint hard and this little yellow snake could just as easily have

been a little yellow prancing horse on the fender of a red Ferrari endurance racer. The white cars also had blue leather accenting the steering wheel, shifter, and handbrake lever; the red/yellow combo included red leather on the same interior pieces.

The five-spoke wheels that were such a hit on the GTS show cars became standard production pieces for 1996 RT/10s. They were silver on black cars, white for white models, and the aforementioned yellow on the red ones. All roadsters (and the GTS) got new rolling stock as well. Though the sizes remained the same, Michelin designed its new Pilot SX MXX3 tires for improved performance, wet or dry. They were also a bit lighter than the previous XGT Z tires.

If there's one thing the Viper needed, even for a

hard-core roadster, it was improved weather protection and a real top for when *al fresco* was not the preferred method of travel. Though several aftermarket companies offered hardtops almost immediately after introduction, Team Viper chose to offer a factory optional unit for 1996. It also fit the previous models. The previous zip-out plastic side curtains gave way to sliding glass units, which could be used with the hardtop or the soft top. Much better.

Many of the 1996-model improvements were found beneath the skin, such as a reviewed chassis that is even torsionally stiffer than the original. The new exhaust also reduced back pressure, so the power and torque ratings increased to 415 horsepower and 488 ft-lb, respectively. A power-steering cooler was added. Other driveline revisions included a new windage tray for the engine, a stronger differential that is more stiffly mounted to the chassis, and uprated drive shafts.

The big change to the suspension system involved cast-aluminum control arms and knuckles to replace the previous steel and cast-iron pieces. The change of material yielded a weight reduction of approximately 60 pounds. The rear roll center was lowered slightly and the suspension geometry was revised to reduce changes during suspension travel; the rear caster angle was also revised. Pickup points for the suspension were relocated to increase the effective shock-absorber travel; higher-rate springs (18 percent rear, 12 percent front) and revised shock-absorber valving were also specified. A recalibrated power-brake booster provided easier pedal modulation, as some owners and media road testers complained that the brakes were a bit too touchy.

All of the above worked together to not only increase overall handling limits, but also to improve control as the Viper neared its handling limits. The car had often been criticized as being too quick to "break away" at the limit of adhesion. Having driven a 1996 with the new suspension hardware and calibration, I can say it felt more progressive, communicative, and controllable than did the earlier Vipers—an improvement to what was already a fine handling sports car.

1996 represented a year of important change for the Viper, as it melded design cues from both the 1992 to 1995 cars, and the 1997 to 2002 machines that were on the horizon. Here you'll notice that the sidepipes have given way to rear-exiting dual exhausts. A factory-engineered hardtop is offered for the first time, though the removable side curtains remained for one more year. *DaimlerChrysler*

THREE

The GTS Coupe, and an Updated RT/10 1997–2002

GTS Coupe

As noted, the Viper GTS Coupe was far more than just a quick, hardtopped re-skin of the RT/10 roadster. Though the look was certainly Viper, there were numerous detail changes to the exterior—so many that it's really a different car. Also, Chrysler's marketing position for the GTS Coupe was more luxury-oriented than with the roadster, in keeping with the *gran turismo* notion represented by the GT portion of its name.

This dashing RT/10 Viper is complete with the new color combinations that were added in 1996. While some traditionalists prefer the single color scheme, the race-inspired stripes became a distinct GST Coupe feature. *Wes Allison*

The front fascia was a different unit, as were the driving lights, and of course the entire rear treatment was designed for the coupe. A race-inspired aluminum quick-fill cap sprouted from the passenger-side sail panel, and the top itself had two gentle bulges to improve head (or helmet?) room. Louvers sprouted along the crest of the front fenderline, just above the wheels. The wheel design made it from prototype to production virtually unchanged and was offered in a polished-only finish. A particularly neat touch was the Viper-logo-shaped, center-mounted stoplight. All glass was tinted, and the rear window opened hatch-style.

Did we say glass? There's more of it on the GTS: a closed coupe body meant side windows, power-actuated no less. With this evolution came door handles; lock/unlock was handled electronically via the key fob. The GTS cockpit received Viper's first interior remodeling. The dash was of a different instrument and control layout, and featured dual air bags. Credit Chrysler's interior designs for an exceptionally handsome integration of these safety devices. Even the air bag–equipped steering wheel still retained a proper sporty look. Revised leather seats included a pump-up lumbar-support feature, and a more powerful stereo system included a CD player.

GTSs also had big news under the hood: a virtually complete redesign of the Viper V-10, which was about 80 pounds lighter than the original, and was rated at 450 horsepower and 490 ft-lb of torque. Head and block castings were new, and eliminated the aforementioned coolant delivery tubes outside the engine. A lighter forged crankshaft rode in cross-bolted main bearings.

The NACA duct in the hood was part of a cold-air intake system, which comprised new manifolding, a redesigned air-filter package, and even a water separator to avoid water getting up the GTS's nose. All of the suspension changes made to the 1996 RT/10 carried over to the GTS. The only color combination offered at launch was metallic blue with white stripes.

Almost from its 1993 concept car premier, the Dodge Viper GTS Coupe has been stealing attention from its open-topped brother, the RT/10 roadster. With its Daytona Cobra Coupe shape, and

Prepare for launch: the new GTS Coupe entered the lineup in mid-1996, joining the revised-for-1997 RT/10 roadster. *DaimlerChrysler*

the possibility of it having more power than the original Viper, the wait for the GTS seemed agonizingly long. GTS production began in May 1996, with about 1,700 coupes built that year.

The RT/10 had not exactly been sitting still, either literally or figuratively. A refresher: the 1992 to 1995 cars may be considered first series Vipers, the ones with three spoke wheels, sidepipes, and the original 400 horsepower V-10. 1996 was a crossover model, as the Viper picked up the GTS's revised fully-independent suspension, frame, 5-spoke wheels, and rear exiting exhaust system. The engine was rated at 415 horsepower, the increase courtesy of the new pipes. 1996 was a limited-build year, as Viper production moved to a new facility as part of the tool-up for GTS.

For 1997, the RT/10 got the rest of the GTS's benefits package, and it made the car both faster and

An early 1992 photograph of a Viper GTS Coupe styling study. This clay mockup used standard RT/10 sidepipes, which were not used on GTS prototypes, and standard Viper wheels. The "double-bubble" roofline was already part of the mix. *DaimlerChrysler*

Above and opposite: It doesn't take a long look at the Peter Brock-designed Shelby Cobra Daytona Cobra Coupe to understand the inspiration for the GTS. Although the Viper was first developed as a street machine, the Cobra was first and foremost a racecar. ***Opposite bottom:*** Carroll Shelby joins former Chrysler VP of Engineering Francois Castaing at the Los Angeles auto show introduction of the GTS Coupe concept. *Above: DaimlerChrysler, opposite top: Wes Allison*

easier to live with. The RT's new 8.0-liter aluminum V-10 shared much of the architecture and design with the original 400/415 horsepower version. One of Viper's original bragging rights was its place as a true roadster, complete with side curtains, no door handles, and a vestigial soft top design that was so difficult to use, you would swear Chrysler made it that way on purpose so it would never be installed. Rollup windows, wet weather protection, and security? That's all for sissies, right? Well, not anymore. A composite hardtop was now standard (as of the 1996 model), although it could be customer-deleted for a savings of $2,500. It was revised in 1997 for a bit more head

room, and worked in concert with the new sideglass windows that made the cabin quieter, and, for the first time, securable.

Windows? In a real roadster? Yes. And all but the most hard core agreed they were a great improvement. The RT/10 got the power windows and indeed the entire door panel setup from the GTS. Along with windows came (you guessed it) door handles. A neat electronic door-actuator button was integrated into a nicely styled, somewhat retro-looking door pull handle. There were no exterior door keylocks; that chore was left strictly to a remote actuator on the key fob.

Several other GTS interior accouterments showed up in the roadster. For the safety minded, the redesigned dash had dual air bags. Credit Chrysler's interior stylists for a commendable job of integrating the air bag into the steering wheel boss; it's not as slick as the leather covered, three-spoke racing wheel found in the previous roadster, but it's Viper-specific, and as handsome as could be expected.

In the best racing tradition, the new pedal assembly was adjustable; a knob mounted beneath the steering column allowed four inches of adjustment. This, combined with the Viper's tilt wheel and exceptionally comfortable leather sport seats (which themselves had another 5.2 inches of travel), meant just about anyone could get comfortable. Air conditioning came full circle: it was not offered on the earliest cars, then became standard, and was now also offered as a delete option (a savings of $1000).

Those who feared the added creature comforts and revisions to the Viper's suspension would tame its earlier reputation as a somewhat hair-trigger oversteer needn't have worried. The driving experience still delivered undiluted, industrial strength performance.

The GTS-spec motor not only made more beans than the previous generation V-10, but it was a bit smoother in the process. Power could be found anywhere on the tach, and the torque curve was as flat as the deck of an aircraft carrier. Dumping the sidepipes

Chrysler made plans for a first-year run of approximately 1,700 GTS Coupes. More than 2/3 of that total were snapped up by existing RT/10 owners. MSRP for the 1996 GTS Coupe was $66,700, a little less than $10,000 more than a roadster—plus gas-guzzler and luxury taxes. Don't let the power windows and CD player fool you into believing the Viper had gone soft. The GTS featured a substantially revised engine rated at 450 horsepower, only about 75 fewer ponies than the base engine in the GTS-R racer. *DaimlerChrysler*

Striking from any angle, the GTS melds the look of the RT/10 and the early 1960s Cobra Daytona Coupe perfectly. NACA hood scoop is functional, and was part of 450-horse V-10's revised intake system. *Bill Delaney, courtesy DaimlerChrysler*

and routing the exhaust out the back was the best thing Chrysler's muffler chefs ever did, and the delicious exhaust note spat out just the right amount of pops and burbles when you backed off the gas. There were others about as fast—the Porsche 911 Turbo comes to mind—but nothing else accelerated with the resolute rightness of the Viper V-10's naturally aspirated cubic inches.

True to form, no automatic transmission was available, with the Borg-Warner T-56 6-speed remaining the only option. Viper's handling improved over the generations, and with the 1997 and later cars, struck a smart balance between rewarding the talented pilot, yet keeping the casual driver from getting in too much trouble. As noted, the earlier cars offered very sharp turn in, and could be provoked into

All Vipers are special, but some, even more so

There have been several "special edition" Vipers offered along the way, but two of the most interesting were based on the GTS Coupe.

The first was the GT2 Championship Edition Viper. It was minted as a 1998 model to commemorate winning the 1997 FIA GT2 Driver's and Manufacturer's Championships. Its color scheme of white with blue stripes acknowledged the look of those factory GTS-R racers and provided a celebratory dichotomy to that of the Shelby Daytona Cobra Coupes, which raced in blue-with-white-striped livery. Though the Championship Edition Viper wore "GTS-R" badges, it is most commonly referred to as the GT2.

This was no mere "paint and stripes" package, however. A revised intake system was good for an extra 10 horsepower, for a total of 460, making it the most powerful Viper sold up to that time. It was also the first Viper to wear factory 18-inch rolling stock, in the form of stunning one-piece BBS alloys and Michelin SX-MXX3 tires. The look was really completed with the addition of a tall rear wing, again resembling that of the real GTS racer, but trimmed "flat" for zero lift or downforce.

The standard black interior was accented with blue trim, including 5-point safety harnesses identical to those of the race car. The obligatory plaque listed the car's VIN and recognized it as one of the limited edition GT2s. MSRP was $85,200, and with only 100 built, they were sold out immediately. Today, the GT2 remains one of the most collectible Vipers ever built, and this author's personal favorite.

Another special, though less limited, edition is the ACR, for American Club Racer. This lighter-weight, somewhat de-contented Viper is for those who really intend to do some club-level racing—or at least want to give that impression.

Introduced in 1999, it picked up some of the hardware first used on the GT2 Championship Edition Coupe; particularly its 18-inch BBS wheels, freer-breathing intake system with

This 1999 model was easily distinguishable from a standard GTS, as were all ACRs, by its BBS "lacey spoke" wheels, and the use of plastic vents instead of fog lights in the front fascia. *DaimlerChrysler*

K&N air filter, and 5-point restraint harnesses. Koni racing shocks and Meritor springs replace the stock units. These changes, when combined with the more aggressive rolling stock, gave the ACR a more-firmly controlled suspension, with only a slight penalty in ride quality.

There wasn't a lot of fat that Dodge could trim from the car without major reprogramming of its engine management or electrical systems, but the front fog lights were deleted in favor of vents. The standard air conditioning and audio system bit the dust too, though they remained optional. For the 2000 model year, the ACR was equipped with high performance oil pan, Dynamic Suspensions adjustable shock absorbers, and wore revised ACR badging.

Like the GT2, the ACR boasted a 460-horsepower rating, and was offered from 1999 through the 2001 model years.

The resemblance is astonishing, by design: Viper GT2 Championship Edition on track with the real thing, a factory GTS-R racer. Note use of similar rear wing. *DaimlerChrysler*

trailing throttle oversteer with little difficulty. The retuned suspension took a bit of that edge off but remained top drawer all the way, and the stiffer frame and lighter suspension components made for greater handling consistency. Handling limits were way up there and a good bit of the credit goes to Michelin's Pilot SX MXX3 Z-rated tires, which were specially configured for Viper duty.

Though 1997's $66,900 MSRP was not cheap for any car under any circumstances, Viper still represented a performance bargain. Purchasing the aforementioned Porsche Turbo would have flattened your wallet by nearly twice as much, and while the Acura NSX delivered higher tech and a more polished handling performance, it too was more expensive and just didn't haul the mail like the big bad Dodge. If anything, America's original, the Corvette, gave the Viper its best run for the money.

The Viper's cabin received substantial revisions with the advent of the GTS Coupe, and they were also engineered into the much-revised 1997 RT/10. The main differences were driver and passenger side air bags and higher quality materials, with power side windows replacing the previous removable side curtains. *Wes Allison*

The new-for-1997 Viper looked little different from the 1996, though the addition of solenoid-actuated door handles was one detail change. *Wes Allison*

Though the C5 didn't quite have the Viper's accelerating ability, it's certainly no slouch, and it had a nicer interior, exceptional handling, and maintained a significant price advantage.

Chrysler continued to evolve the Viper throughout that generation's six-year production life. Naturally, colors, trim, and wheel finishes were freshened just about every year. Numerous "special editions" were offered too (see sidebar). The air bag systems were updated for 1998, and a passenger side on/off switch was added. In 1999 came new 18-inch wheels across the board, and an optional Connolly leather-trimmed interior. Big news for Viper owners with families came along in 2000 in the form of child seat tethers. Team Viper finally acknowledged that a well-developed and properly calibrated anti-lock braking system would be a benefit to most drivers and would do nothing to dilute the Viper's no-holds-barred persona, so ABS was made standard beginning with the 2001 model year.

Looking back, it's clear that the 1997 to 2002 model years were the Viper's most successful. Two distinct models and numerous special editions were offered, and the car continued to evolve and improve while it also remained a strong seller, even into its 10th production year. Dodge released the 2002 Viper GTS Final Edition on July 1, 2002, as the team and assembly plant began preparations to produce the new Viper SRT-10 that would bow for 2003.

Right: Who would argue with 50 more horsepower? Nobody, and that's what the GTS and 1997-and-later RT/10s got. Although the engine's architecture remained the same, there were many detail improvements, especially in terms of block rigidity and cooling. It was essentially a new engine.

The end of the road, or at least the end of another chapter in the Viper's book of life. DaimlerChrysler workers marked the last 2002 special Dodge Viper GTS "Final Edition" with a brief ceremony as the vehicle was driven from the assembly line at the Conner Avenue Assembly Plant in July of that year. The Coupe, which represented the last of 360 Viper GTS models built on the 2002 Viper platform, carries the Vehicle Identification Number 102736. *Joe Wilssens, courtesy DaimlerChrysler*

FOUR

Record Breaking: Vipers on Track

I t's the oldest saw in the business: "Win on Sunday, Sell on Monday." One look at the GTS tells you it was meant to be a race car. As discussed, it was clearly cast in the mold of the Cunninghams and Cobra Daytona Coupes of the past, so Chrysler elected to take the obvious step: make a race version. The GTS-R is a limited-production, factory-developed racing Viper that was offered for sale to private teams. Chrysler also fielded its own factory-backed team—to great success as we'll see.

The ultimate triumph: the Beretta/Dupuy/Wendlinger Team ORECA Viper GTS-R on its way to a stunning overall victory in the 2000 Rolex 24 Hours of Daytona, just one of its many important sports car wins and championships. *DaimlerChrysler*

The GTS-R was designed to compete in international GT-class competition, homologated for ACO, IMSA/ALMS, and FIA events. According to Bob Lutz, "This is a no-holds-barred competition car care for the world's great events such as the 24 Hours of Daytona and the 24 Hours of Le Mans. It is . . . perhaps the only [production-derived racing car] developed, produced, and sold directly from an American manufacturer through its own organization. Honchoing the development of the GTS-R was Team Viper member (and SCCA national driving champ) Neil Hanneman, and the development partner/supplier Reynard Racing Cars, a highly successful constructor for several racing series such as IndyCar and F3. The GTS-R was introduced to the media in August 1995 at the Pebble Beach Lodge in Monterey, California.

The basic GTS Coupe's steel space frame was retained and strengthened via CAD design enhancements and the integration of a roll-cage structure. Exterior coachwork maintained most of the stock car's dimensions, but the GTS-R body is rendered in carbon fiber. One must wonder how many GTS-R-styled rear wings will end up on street Vipers. The carbon-fiber dash panel carried standard instrumentation, and an otherwise stripped interior also contained an on-board fire-extinguisher system.

For power, special dry-sump versions of the V-10 were constructed in three different states of tune with

The No. 97 Sifton/Robinson/Seibert GTS-R at the GTS-R's second competition outing at the Sebring 12 Hours of Endurance Race in March 1996. *G. Hewitt, DaimlerChrysler*

Wind tunnel testing of the aerodynamics of the GTS-R. A story in *AutoWeek* magazine discussed some of the GTS-R's early teething problems, but this was to be expected with any new racing program. Further development to the GTS-R's shape and cooling made the car more stable and reliable at speed, necessary for both the long straights at Le Mans, and the high banks of Daytona. *DaimlerChrysler*

factory offered ratings of 525, 650, and 700 horsepower; the base version was engineered in-house by Team Viper; the latter two were developed in cooperation with Caldwell Development Inc. A racing version of the production Borg-Warner T-56 six-speed manual helped deliver power through an alloy-cased Dana rear end. A combination of stock and specially built pieces composed the suspension, and Michelin racing slicks, BBS modular wheels, and Brembo disc brakes rounded out the rolling stock. All yours for a mere $200,000. Unfortunately, we don't have the space to delve into the various privateer teams that race GTS-Rs and so have chosen to stick primarily with the factory-sponsored efforts.

The GTS-R got its first taste of competition in the 1996 Rolex 24 Hours of Daytona. Running in the GT-1 class, the Canaska/Southwind Racing Vipers demonstrated class-leading speed in practice qualifying 17th and 30th overall. The No. 97 Sifton/Robinson/Seibert entry was involved in an accident on lap 157 and retired. The Cobb/Dismore/Hendricks No. 98 GTS-R battled with transmission and braking problems throughout the race, but it was running at the end and finished 29th overall. Not exactly a win, but an honest showing for an all-new car, and the lessons learned began to show the GTS-R's development program where they needed to go. Four Vipers were entered at Le Mans in

Here is an important group of men in the Viper's history. From left: Bud Liebler, former Chrysler vice president of marketing and communications; Marty Levine, former Dodge Division general manager; Roy Sjoberg, former executive engineer of Team Viper; Tony George, president, Indianapolis Motor Speedway; Neil Hanneman, project manager, Viper GTS-R; Tom Gale and Francois Castaing, two of the Vipers Fourfathers. This photo was taken at the Viper GTS-R's introduction in August 1995.

1996, two by Canaska and two by the French Team ORECA. That result was also credible, if not all-conquering: 8th, 12th, and 14th in class, plus a DNF. That might be considered what stick-and-ball teams dub "a building year."

Chrysler got more serious with its own factory-backed GTS-R racing program in 1997 but needed to engage a world class partner to compete at the highest levels. In spite of the fact that the genesis of the GTS-R and its early development were very much Chrysler factory programs, it still took a great team

to "teach a car how to race." Team Penske was one of the best examples of an organization that built team infrastructure, attracted top quality drivers, executed a proper testing program, and just "knew the ropes" come race day. Reinhold Joest, whose teams and drivers pulled off Audi's back-to-back-to-back wins at the Le Mans, was another. In NASCAR terms, think Robert Yates Racing, DEI, or Roush Enterprises.

Chrysler found its "Penske" in the form of Hughes de Chaunac and his Team ORECA, which had campaigned two Vipers at Le Mans in 1996. De Chaunac

The Viper GTS-R interior is all business. The dash resembles the shape of the new GTS Coupe unit, but the GTS-R's dash is rendered in carbon fiber. The red handles to the lower right are for the on-board fire-extinguisher system. *DaimlerChrysler*

had already achieved considerable success since winning Team ORECA's first European F2 championship in 1975 and masterminding Mazda's overall Le Mans victory in 1991, to name a few highlights. Team ORECA was experienced in international sports car racing, capable, and available. De Chaunac and company would field Chrysler's expanded factory effort in international sports car racing, running for the FIA GT Championship series, at Le Mans, and, ultimately, in the American Le Mans and Grand Am

This GTS-R engine rendering shows the dry sump and the long tube exhaust headers; it was based on the new GTS Coupe V-10, and was rated at 525 horsepower in base form. As raced during the 2000 season, its output, after considerable development, was more like 750. *DaimlerChrysler*

series. The results rewrote the sports car racing record books.

Though the Team ORECA Vipers did not capture that much sought-after Le Mans class victory in 1997, finishing 5th and 6th in the GT2 class, they did win the FIA GT2 championship, with Justin Bell taking the driver's title. This important European series championship provided the inspiration for the 1998 GT2 Championship Edition Viper.

The year 1998 proved to be the first of three record-breaking, watershed years for the GTS-R. Not only did Team ORECA repeat as the FIA GT2 champions, they bagged that all-important 1-2 class victory at Le Mans. Justin Bell, Luca Drudi, and David Donohue led the effort, with Oliver Beretta, Tommy Archer, and Pedro Lamy completing the 1-2 finish. Two privateer Vipers finished 5th and 7th in class, demonstrating without doubt that the Viper could withstand 24 hours of punishment and had matured into a fast and reliable race car.

This success continued virtually unabated during the 1999 season, in spite of the team adding another dimension to its competition efforts. Don Panoz had taken over the World Sports Car series and rebuilt it around the same rules employed by the ACO at Le Mans. The sports car racing formula that was so

Success at last: the Justin Bell/Donohue/Drudi GTS-R in the pits at Le Mans, 1998, on the way to its first class victory at the all-important French Classic.

The First Viper Road Racer

Strange as it may seem, there was Viper racing before the creation of the GTS-R. An early 1990s reformulation of various GT classes by the ACO opened the door for entries like the Viper. Oddly enough, it was a privateer French team that was first to build one for Le Mans in 1994. LMGT-1 class rules provide for few modifications, and the Rent-A-Car race team's two Vipers were amazingly stock. The cars ran with hardtops and performed well considering the Viper's lack of racing development at the time and the team's limited budget. Intermittent transmission overheating and other niggling problems prevented a class win, but the cars finished 12th and 18th overall. The red No. 40 car's 12th place run, courtesy of Bertrand Balas, Justin Bell, and former F1 ace Rene Arnoux, was also good enough for a 3rd place in class.

Photo finish: Olivier Beretta, Karl Wendlinger, and Dominique Dupuy cross the line to take the class win at Le Mans, 1999, with the Archer/Bell/Duez GTS-R coming home a close second.

successful in Europe had been brought to America; the result was the American Le Mans Series (ALMS). Since the Viper was already a proven winner and America was, of course, its home market, Chrysler elected to not only continue participating in the FIA GT series and at Le Mans, but to add ALMS as well.

The Team ORECA Vipers achieved every goal put in front of them in 1999. They took the FIA GT championship for a third consecutive year and repeated their 1998 Le Mans performance with another impressive 1-2 finish in the renamed GTS category. This time it was Olivier Beretta, Karl Wendlinger, and Dominique Dupuy crossing the line first, with the Archer/Bell/Duez GTS-R coming home second. Even though it entered the 1999 ALMS season late (running only six races) Beretta claimed the GTS class driver's title and ORECA the team

title, and Viper only narrowly missed the constructor's crown for Dodge.

Team ORECA had become such an integral part of the GTS-R's development that Chrysler's Motorsport division appointed Hughes de Chaunac as the car's exclusive constructor and distributor at the end of 1998. This meant that customers could virtually buy the same car as the factory entered.

As if the 1999 season hadn't proven the GTS-R and Team ORECA's worth, the Chrysler/de Chaunac juggernaut added yet another challenge for 2000: the Rolex 24 Hours of Daytona. The Grand Am series had been formed as a competitor to the ALMS, and its crown jewel was the 24-hour enduro in Florida. Further challenge was on the horizon in the form of an increasingly competitive, factory-backed Chevrolet Corvette C5-R effort. Nonetheless, Chrysler, the

Call it a threepeat, hat trick, whatever you like. The 1999 class winners, Olivier Beretta, Karl Wendlinger, and Dominique Dupuy, backed up Team ORECA's previous year's win and made it three in a row for the GTS-R in the GT2/GTS category at Le Mans.

team, the renamed Viper GTS-R/T, and a proven roster of drivers took it all on.

It's rare that a production-based sports car like the Viper stands much of a chance against purpose-built prototypes for an overall victory, especially in a longer event, where the faster, higher-tech machines' lead generally continues to increase as the hours click away. Yet, 24 hours is a long time, and as the saying goes, "anything can happen in racing." Well, anything and everything did at the Rolex 24 Hours on February 5 and 6, 2000. Many of the new Grand Am spec prototypes were yet unproven. Conversely, the GTS-R had benefited from years of development, and tens of thousands of miles of track time and testing.

The GTS-R's freight train–like reliability plus solid driving by Olivier Beretta, Karl Wendlinger, and

Dominique Dupuy—and an inordinate amount of teething problems and accidents suffered by many of the faster prototype class machines—allowed the No. 91 Viper GTS-R to claim a historic overall victory (plus, obviously, the GTO class win) at Daytona. The tables were so turned in Florida that year that the highest finishing prototype came home fourth. The Fellows/Bell/Kneifel Corvette C5-R finished a credible second (losing to Wendlinger in the Viper by just 30 seconds), with Team ORECA's Donohue/Ni Amorim/Belloc/Archer GTS-R finishing third overall. Amazing, and without doubt, the GTS-R's finest hour in competition to date.

Wendlinger, Beretta, and Dupuy kicked off the 2000 ALMS in fine style, notching the Viper's first win at the 12 Hours of Sebring. With the Sebring and

Daytona wins under its belt, the next goal for the now-red Vipers was to make history again with a "threepeat" at Le Mans—and so they did. The same driver threesome finished first in the GTS class at Le Mans, with the Donohue/Ni Amorim/Beltoise GTS-R/T coming in second this time.

Team ORECA went on to win the ALMS championship for 2000, a season that saw the GTS-R/T take sports car racing's "Triple Crown" in the form of class wins at Le Mans, Sebring, and Daytona, plus the overall win at the latter. During its four year, factory-backed stay in international sports car racing, Team ORECA won 44 races in FIA GT, ALMS, ACO, and Grand Am competition, not to mention numerous driver, team, and constructor championships, plus class or overall victories in the world's most significant sports car races. Team patron Hughes de Chaunac summarized his feelings and the team's accomplishments by saying "We have had a lot of success with this car. Now, it will go into the history book as one of the most successful racing cars of its era, and I am quite honored to have been a part of this history."

Thumbs up guys, for a production-based sports car taking an overall win at Daytona in 2000. From left, drivers Karl Wendlinger and Olivier Beretta, Chrysler competition manager Lou Patane, Team ORECA patron Hughes de Chaunac, and third teammate Dominique Dupuy. *DaimlerChrysler*

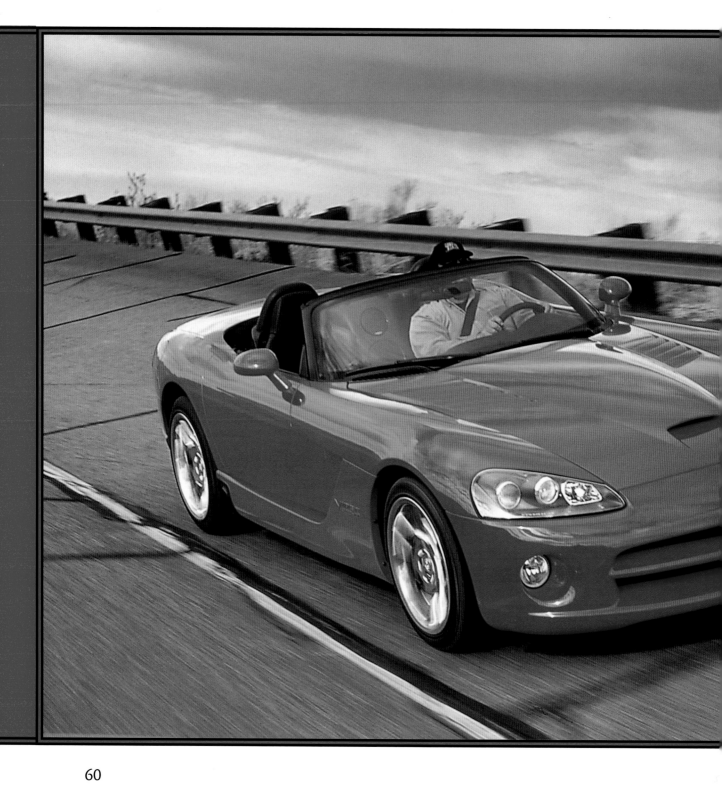

FIVE

Vipers for a New Millenium: The 2003 SRT-10 and Beyond

Dodge likes to talk about the SRT-10's three 500s—actually, the new Viper's specs are 500 horsepower, 525 ft-lb of torque, and 505 cubic inches. But we're not going to get persnickety with Dodge. These are impressive numbers, any way you make them.

As beloved as the original Viper was—it evolved continuously, but remained architecturally un-changed for the decade it was on the market—it was time for a new one. Enough had been learned about the car's shortcomings, and the wish list was getting long. After the revised 1997 RT-10 and GTS were launched, Chrysler management and Team Viper got to thinking about where they could take the car from there.

There's no mistaking the SRT-10 for anything but a Viper, although the evolution between the two is anything but subtle. All of the proportions have changed, as has the detailing, intake and exhaust vent shapes, and more. Dual HID headlights are seriously bright, and the hood scoop delivers intake air directly into the dual air cleaner system. The author is at the wheel. *Wes Allison*

They spent a good six months conceptualizing, talking, and arguing about what the car ought, and ought *not*, to be. According to comments from several team members and executives, the main challenges were how to update the look, yet have the car still be pure Viper, and how to make the car more sophisticated (and comfortable) without diluting its visceral, raw appeal.

One goal everyone was clear and united on was another horsepower increase. Tom Gale, original Viper Fourfather and Chrysler design director, was quoted in Daniel F. Carney's *Dodge Viper* as saying "We are going to keep our lace in the queue; if that means 500 horsepower and 500 foot-pounds of torque,

then that's what it will be. If it means that we've got to do things that will give it the capability of being the benchmark in terms of slalom, if it means we've got to keep it at the top of the heap in braking, if it means all those things, then that's what we'll do."

"Five hundred has always been a magic number," continued John Fernandez, executive engineer. He was ultimately in charge of the Viper project, and director of DaimlerChrysler's newly created Performance Vehicles Operations (PVO). "It's been a performance target for Viper and the Specialty Vehicles Engineering Team for years." Team Viper member Brian Cojocari was manager of the new program, which was given the internal development

Designer Osamu Shikado's rendering of the GTS-R concept of 2000 (inspired by, but not to be confused with, the race car of the same name) embodies the design cues that would show up on the SRT-10 production roadster a few years later. Is this a long-lead look at a future GTS? We say yes. *DaimlerChrysler*

TV to SVE to PVO

In the early 1990s, Ford elected to gather its various high performance skunkworks entities together under one banner, in order to develop performance-oriented versions of mainstream production models. The group was named the Special Vehicle Team, or SVT. Nobody knows why it took both GM and Chrysler a decade to do the same, but it finally happened: GM now has the General Motors Performance Division (GMPD) and Chrysler has its Performance Vehicle Operations, or PVO. Luckily enough, PVO already had a poster child in house—the Viper, of course—and annexed what was Team Viper (which by then fell under the banner of Special Vehicle Engineering) into the group.

As the SRT-10 was being developed, original Team Viper leader Roy Sjoberg retired and was replaced by John Fernandez. Fernandez, a performance and motorsports enthusiast to the core, was also called upon to lead the new organization; the formalization of PVO was announced to the public in January of 2002.

Fernandez' tenure as PVO boss was short, as he was soon tapped to concentrate fully on the Chrysler Group's motorsports activities, including the NASCAR effort, parts programs, SCCA, and the like. "The same engineers that recently dominated the worldwide GT scene with the Viper GTS-R now have their sights set on the Winston Cup. My job is to get them the resources they need to be successful, and I'm going to do that," Fernandez explained. But he was around long enough to make an indelible mark on PVO, as he oversaw the development of the Viper Competition Coupe.

Dan Knott took over PVO's reigns in the fall of 2002 and remains the group's director as of this writing. It's important to understand the scope of PVO. Unlike the original Team Viper, which was a group of individuals highly focused on a single project, PVO will develop performance variants for not only Dodge, but Chrysler and Jeep branded vehicles. PVO also has responsibility for Mopar Performance Parts, but most importantly for readers of this book, is charged with continuing to develop the Viper SRT-10.

PVO Motorsport Director and all around performance guru, John Fernandez. *DaimlerChrysler*

GTS-R concept's interior was obviously the springboard for what the production SRT-10s cabin would look like. Dodge did a good job of "productionizing" the dream machine's look, retaining the instrument panel layout and similar splashes of aluminum trim. *DaimlerChrysler*

code name VGX.

Enthusiasts got a preview of the 2003 Viper SRT-10 as the Viper GTS-R concept car, not to be confused with the racing Viper of the same name, at the 2000 International Auto Show in Detroit. This was the same venue at which the original Viper concept car had created a production life and legend for itself a little more than a decade earlier. It didn't take a lot of imagination to see that this "concept" was being developed as a show toy to introduce the new production Viper to the public and the media.

There were differences, of course. The GTS-R was presented as a coupe, although the SRT-10 would debut only as a roadster. The concept's interior also foretold the SRT-10's cabin, but most of the expensive materials wouldn't make the mix, although the instrument panel design and some of the aluminum trim ultimately did.

The chassis retained its predecessor's basic architecture, but it had been stretched and updated. The all-new framework on the wish list didn't make the program due to cost restraints, but the SRT-10 was still approximately 35 percent torsionally stiffer and about 40 pounds lighter than before. The wheelbase

This cutaway drawing shows the SRT-10 in final production form, and from the inside out. Sport roof bar gave way to a clean rear deck; the Viper's greater rear track and longer wheelbase are easily noticeable from this angle. *David Kimball, courtesy DaimlerChrysler*

Another important element that separates the SRT-10 from the RT/10 is the use of a conventional convertible top. It does away with the need for a removable hardtop or soft top, and in the case of the early cars, side curtains. Some like the look better, while others prefer the previous design. *Wes Allison*

increased by 2.6 inches, resulting in a more commodious cabin. And the SRT-10 wore bigger tires than ever: 275/35ZR18s on 18x10-inch wheels up front, with steamroller-inspired 345/30ZR19s wrapped around 19x13-inch alloys out back.

Sidepipes returned, an original Viper design cue that had gone away in 1996. Brembo four-wheel disc brakes with ABS were standard and represented an engineering advance on the ABS-equipped system

introduced in 2001. Overall vehicle weight went down by about 80 pounds, though it's still kind of porky by sports-car-purist standards; all the safety, emissions, and convenience stuff demanded by today's government and marketplace conditions add tonnage.

There was a lot of talk among current Viper owners and in the media about the Viper's new design and the work of talented staff designer Osamu

Continued on page 68

2003 Viper Comp Coupe

"Ambitious, yet extremely logical," says John Fernandez, director of Dodge Motorsports operations.

Taking the new Dodge Viper roadster and making a full race coupe out of it was ambitious. While there are plenty of high-performance parts in the SRT-10 street car, there was still loads of work to do to make the Viper a turnkey racer. Logical, Fernandez says, because there's a ready market. After all, dozens of Viper racers were taking a new $80,000 car and throwing away $30,000 worth of safety and comfort equipment—air bags, climate control, seats, stereo, you name it—and spending thousands more to make their cars raceable.

So Fernandez and crew took the platform and basic powertrain of the Viper roadster and built their own racer.

We're talking an FIA-legal rollcage, onboard telemetry, a sectioned composite body of Kevlar, carbon fiber, and fiberglass, with front splitters and a rear wing developed in a wind tunnel. And did we mention pneumatic jacks, a fire-suppression system, a Racetech seat with a six-point harness, three-piece BBS wheels with Hoosier racing slicks, Brembo brakes with carbon-fiber cooling ducts, Moton adjustable coil-over dampers, a 25-gallon fuel cell, and electronically adjustable brake bias? For just $100,000 or so.

Two Viper Competition Coupes, flying the PVO banner, at the car's media test program in January 2003. The Coupe won its first Speed Challenge race before the end of that year, and must represent the ultimate club racer. *DaimlerChrysler*

Given the level of sophistication, it's pointed out to Fernandez there's no way he could be making money at that price. He doesn't disagree. What, sell at a loss, and make it up in volume?

No, make it up in parts. Though the Viper Competition Coupe should be exceptionally durable, plans are that each will lead a long and happy life and, as such, will require periodic maintenance, body-panel replacement, that sort of thing. It's something the razor-blade companies learned decades ago: we'll give you a free razor—if you keep buying our blades.

Even so, only the first 32 lucky customers got the $100,000 price. The next 30 or so cars cost $118,000, and the eventual price will settle in at about $125,000. Viper Club of America members, many of whom are avid racers, got first shot. Sales are directly from Dodge—local dealers aren't involved. How hard would it be to make that thing street legal? Unfortunately, the answer is, "very hard." Example: what appears to be headlights are decals. This is a racetrack-only car, folks.

That's the bad news. The good news: it isn't that much

Though the Comp Coupe's engine remains internally stock, it does benefit from improved intake and exhaust systems. This tubular triangulation brace helps stiffen the chassis, sharpening both handling and steering response. *DaimlerChrysler*

faster than the production Viper roadster, which says a lot for the streeter. Of all the work Fernandez and his Performance Vehicle Operations guys did on the Competition Coupe, the one area left comparatively alone is the powertrain. The stock SRT-10 Viper has a 505-cubic-inch V-10, with 500 horsepower, 500 ft-lb of torque, and a Tremec six-speed manual transmission. The Competition Coupe ups horsepower to 520, torque to 540 ft-lb, and has the same Tremec tranny. Though there are a few engine tweaks, most of the modest power boost comes from the lower-restriction intake and exhaust.

It takes a while to warm up the Competition Coupe's fat Hoosier slicks (P305/35ZR18 front, P345/30ZR18 rear), but once you do, they stick quite well. Like all Vipers before it, this one responds to a rather brutal, off/on switch–like driving style. The tires don't offer much warning before they lose traction, but once they do, the result isn't dramatic. Big four-piston Brembo brakes are astoundingly capable and fade-free, lap after hard lap.

The engine's monstrous torque makes the Competition Coupe easy to drive fast. Exit a corner one gear too high, and the massive V-10 shrugs it off and goes. Redline is around 6,100 rpm, with about 5,400 rpm a comfortable shift point. The biggest surprise is that, after driving the stock roadster and the Comp Coupe, you get the feeling that, if it had slick tires, the stock Viper might be only a couple seconds slower than the Coupe on a road course. That a street-legal car could feel so much like a full-on racer again speaks to the extreme nature of the production Viper.

Dodge's Performance Vehicle Operations planned on producing about 60 Competition Coupes for 2003 and at least that many for 2004. Beyond that, they'll build as many as they can sell.

The car is designed to compete in the Skip Thomas Viper Racing League, as well as the Grand American Cup's Grand Sports class (against the Chevrolet Corvette and Porsche Carrera), and in the Speedvision World Challenge.

Gentlemen, your razor is ready.

—Steven Cole Smith, reprinted courtesy *Motor Trend*

PVO's Manager of Vehicle Synthesis Herb Helbig puts the spurs to a late SRT-10 "pilot" prototype. Although it resembles the production version in most details, it's not quite a finished piece. Note missing nose badge. *Wes Allison*

Shikado (see sidebar). Osamu addressed every detail of the car, including a new logo. Some appreciated that the SRT-10 had a more fully-realized and better-proportioned look than before; others said it wasn't "as visceral" as the 1992 to 2002 models. The original RT/10 was an eye-catcher, for sure, but to this author's eyes, it now looks a little cartoonish next to the fresh shape of the 2003.

A lot of the new Viper's shape was driven by wind tunnel testing. While the original car's tapered tail wasn't aerodynamic and occasionally created some high-speed stability issues, the SRT-10's broad shoulders and upturned tail created effective downforce, and allowed the air to roll more cleanly off the back of the car. High-speed stability was much improved.

The first-generation roadster's sports bar, removable rear window, and hardtop/soft-top combo all gave way to a conventional folding convertible top. Many felt this was better than the old system, especially that of the 1996 and earlier models, with their Erector Set-inspired side curtains and toupee-like soft top. The manual top folds neatly, and employs a glass rear window complete with defroster. No separate cover was necessary—it creates its own as it folds down behind the seats.

The previous Viper's tapered tail contribution did little to support high–speed stability. The SRT-10s rear styling is more aerodynamically efficient and creates measurable downforce that helps keep the rear end better planted. This new '03 design also represented the often-asked-for return to sidepipes, which had gone away at the end of the'95 model run. *Wes Allison*

The 2003 headlight clusters contain Xenon-gas high-intensity-discharge elements for both high and low beam. A car with this sort of performance should never be short of lighting, and the only brighter eyes than these are found on race cars and jet fighters. There's a somewhat European influence to be found in the new car's muscular shoulders and flipping tail. Yet its square jaw, bodacious stance, and overall aggressiveness are all-American, and all-Viper, all the way.

You can talk 440 Six-Packs, L88s, and Boss 429s until you're blue, but the SRT-10's 505-ci/8.3-liter all-aluminum V-10 (carrying the internal project code DVX) may be the meanest big-block ever put into a series production car. (The NASCAR and NHRA cheater motors dropped into a few factory-supported back-door racing projects during the 1960s don't count.) It's good for 500 real SAE net horsepower on premium unleaded pump gas. It was new, right down to the block, and featured a neater throttle-cable setup than before, as well as an effective cold-air-intake system. This power plant represented a 50-horsepower increase over the previous-generation

Viper By Design

It took Osamu Shikado, design manager, DaimlerChrysler Advance Packaging Studio, about five minutes to sketch for us this rendering of his most recent design project—although he worked on the 2003 SRT-10 for much longer than that. The new Viper represents a considerable departure for this Osaka, Japan–born designer; his previous gig was with Toyota, where he worked on all manner of Camrys and Corollas. The Viper GTS-R concept of 2000 was by no means his first design-study project since coming to the United States; he also designed the stunning Chrysler Chronos concept of 1998, and 1999's Chrysler Citadel. The Viper, however, is his magnum opus to date, and he comments that "it's an honor to redesign an American icon."

Viper SRT-10 lead designer Osamu Shikado.

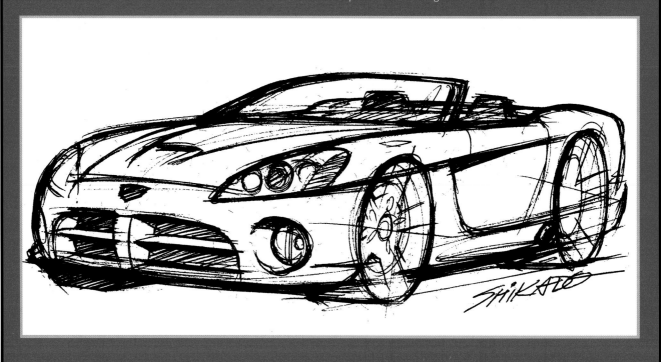

The SRT-10's 8.3-liter (just over 505 cubic inches!) V-10 represents a new high-water mark in terms of domestic production sports car powerplants. It puts out a full 500 horsepower on unleaded fuel, while meeting all emissions and OBD II laws. Although its layout is similar to that of previous Vipers, it's an all-new engine. The most visible features are the dual front snorkel-mounted air filters and neater routing of wiring and throttle linkage. *Wes Allison*

non-ACR-spec V-10. A Tremec T-56 six-speed manual transmission remained your only gear-changing choice. An automatic? Don't even ask.

Hop in, and you'll immediately notice that the pedal box is no longer intruded upon by the front wheelhouse. A large tach now sits front and center, with a smaller speedo just to its right. The rest of the ancillary gauges (oil pressure, oil temp, water temp, and charging system) cascade down the IP just to the right of the steering wheel. There's a new stereo with—you guessed it—500 watts of power; it packs a

six-CD changer and even a speed-sensitive volume mode, as if anyone will even listen to it. From there, it's a simple-to-use HVAC system, power window switches, and that's about it.

The quality of the materials used in the interior increased substantially. Splashes of aluminum and aluminum-look trim brightened the interior, and the new leather sport seats are absolutely superb—comfortable, supportive even during aggressive cornering, and handsome. All in all, a much nicer place to be than the previous Viper's cockpit.

Herb Helbig, Keeper of the Viper Flame

The group that conceives, designs, tests, develops, and builds the Viper has changed a lot since the late 1980s. So how does a big company like DaimlerChrysler (which itself was just plain old "Chrysler" when the car first came out) ensure that a Viper remains true to the concepts and tenets of, well, Viperness? It takes a "Grailkeeper." PVO's is Herb Helbig.

By all accounts, Helbig is the right guy for the job. He's educated, with Masters and Graduate degrees in mechanical engineering, plus a Masters in automotive engineering. He's experienced, having been with Chrysler since 1972, and more importantly, with the Viper program since the very beginning. And he's a total and complete gearhead.

His official title is PVO Manager of Vehicle Synthesis. But what does that really mean? "Keeping the Viper, as it evolves through the course of its life, true to the original set of parameters. We've got to keep it simple, we've got to make it fun, its got to be the most outrageous car you've ever touched. When you turn the key on, the hair on the back of your neck has got to stand up. It's got to be a visceral, emotional, almost religious experience. It falls to me to make sure that we don't lose sight of why we started this program. [It's all about] fun, passion, and the desire just to put people back on their heels to say 'I can't believe these guys made such an outrageous, awesome, off-the-scale car,'" explained Helbig. Clear enough.

Helbig was the fourth person hired by Team Viper's original project leader Roy Sjoberg, and has seen a lot of change since the late 1980s. Yet it is this evolution that ended up defining his job. "It's a challenge to mature it, to grow the car up a little, yet not lose its essence, and to allow an expanding customer base to be satisfied. How do you play to a bigger audience without prostituting yourself. Sometimes it keeps me awake at night, " Helbig said. One such example was the development of power side windows for the GTS, a big departure from the original, windowless RT-10 roadster. The team ultimately felt that the move was necessary, both for the flavor and for the design of the new coupe.

Lest you worry that Helbig is about to let the Viper get soft around the middle: "When people come to me and say 'you know it really needs cruise control; I took one to Chicago and my right foot got kinda tired. . . .' that guy gets thrown out of my office. Or a guy comes in and says 'you know, it would be cool if we had power seats' that guy gets thrown out of the building. And the guy who says 'I think we need an automatic transmission' well, they're still looking for his body."

Herb was involved in every step of the SRT-10s development. High and low points? "The thing I'm most pleased with are the brakes. If you look back to the beginning, we tried to build the car with as many off-the-shelf parts as we could because we had a somewhat limited budget. Our original brake system was awesome for the time—for the street. But we didn't realize how many people were going to beat the car on the race track, and how hard they were going to run them. The system evidenced itself as having some shortcomings for that kind of use. On the new car, we said 'by God we are going to make sure you cannot find a weakness on the brake system of the SRT-10.' You can take an SRT-10, go to the Blackhawk Farms road course, run 25 laps with Tommy Archer in the driver's seat, and not diminish the brakes. It won't boil, it won't fade, it'll just stop."

On the downside? "I wished we done a better job of managing the car's thermal load. The car's hot inside. As you know, we went back to sidepipes, because that's what we

and our customers wanted. It spoke to the heritage of the original car. We took the cats that used to be just in the sill, and we split them up. Under your feet, instead of just having pipe, you have a one-cubic-foot cat that's burning at 1,600 degrees. A smaller cat remains in the sill, but its still a 1,600-degree heat source. In order to get good tonal quality, and pass noise restrictions, we had to create a crossover network, so the pipework from each side of the car crosses over to the other side, right under the passenger seats. We've [got] three sides of each passenger surrounded by the exhaust system [under the floor]. We wish we could have figured out a way to do a better job with that."

The future of domestic performance cars like the Viper? "When you think about the guys in Dearborn [Ford], and the guys in Warren [GM], and us guys in Auburn Hills, and there's a lot pride and bragging rights involved, and there's no way that, when the bar gets raised by one of those three groups, the other guys aren't going to be working over their cauldron, boiling something up that's going to put them back on top.

"We're glad that those guys have taken up the challenge. It allows [us] to go to our management and say 'we can't sit on our laurels and rest on our accomplishments. We've got to keep pushing the envelope.' PVO will stop at nothing to continue to be the king of this hill. You can take that one to the bank. I'm really blessed that I get to do this kinda stuff every day, and get paid for it."

PVO Manager of Vehicle Synthesis and original Team Viper member Herb Helbig. *DaimlerChrysler*

Few would argue that the SRT-10's cabin is a major advancement over the 1992 to 2002 Vipers. The longer wheelbase means less wheelhouse intrusion into the foot box, the instrumentation is easier to see and read, and the aluminum trim lends an upscale, racy look. Seating is improved, as is a new 500-watt audio system. The tach also takes its race car-inspired place—front and center—in the instrument panel. *Wes Allison*

Light the V-10, and once again, you'll hear that rumbling, sputtering hum directly to the left and right of your shoulders. We mentioned the return to sidepipes, in part due to customer feedback and request. The exhaust system on 1992 to 1995 models contained no crossover piping, so each side of the car (effectively) emitted the exhaust noise of a 4.0-liter five-cylinder engine. Most feel the Viper pipebenders did a better job this time around; it's a deeper, richer, nastier thrum, replete with some pops and crackle on the overrun.

Fast? Absolutely. *Motor Trend* achieved a 0 to 60 time of 3.9 seconds; a review of most of its test numbers from years past showed RT/10 test times of between 4.0 to 4.2 seconds. *MT* commented: "The word—other than really fast!—that best describes the rest of the driving experience is 'progressivity.' The previous Viper was anything but: twitchy, quick to break away at the limit, a not-so-easy to modulate clutch, ad infinitum. This one is substantially better and more accurately transmits your brain signals and control inputs into appropriate responses. Steering

One of the many detail changes that differentiate the SRT-10 from the previous generation Vipers is the complete redesign of the hood. On the older cars, it's a one-piece clamshell that includes front fenders. This piece was difficult to align properly and expensive to repair. On the SRT-10, it gives way to a more conventional hood, and the previous "speaker grille" vents are replaced by five slats per side, representing the engine's five-cylinder-per-bank layout. *DaimlerChrysler*

turn-in remains fast and sharp, but is more linear, with good feel. Brakes? Plenty, and again, the system is nicely progressive in the way it hauls the car to a stop; pedal feel and modulation have improved, too. Nose dive under braking was never a problem for the old Viper, nor is it with this one. Ride quality feels a bit more supple than before, though that's not to be interpreted as the Viper being in any way watered down."

Road & Track said, "A gentle push of the red button and the 8.3-liter V-10 rumbles to life, each throaty side pipe sounding off from all 10 cylinders, thanks to the way the exhaust is routed and inter-connected . . . the ghosts of the UPS truck exhaust note have been exorcised and now the Viper has the snarl to match the drivetrain's bite." *R & T* continued: "Several quick tours around the 1.7 mile handling track at [Chrysler's] Chelsea [proving ground] reinforced my earlier impressions of the car as being much more civilized in both ride and handling. And yet, when pushed hard, it could deliver the kind of straight-line thrills that have been a Viper benchmark."

It all came at a price, with the 2003 SRT-10's base MSRP increasing to $83,795.

Performance Comparison
Source: *Motor Trend*, June, 2003

Model	0-60 (sec)	0-100-0 (sec)	1/4-Mile (ET@speed)	Top Speed (mph)	Price (as tested)
Viper SRT-10	3.94	12.17	11.77@123.63	182	$83,795
Ferrari 575M	4.16	13.94	12.26@118.58	182	$241,092
Corvette Z06	4.29	13.92	12.44@116.54	174	$51,450
Lamborghini Murcielago	3.51	12.71	11.72@122.52	193	$284,850

Yet when you consider how expensive it is to add horsepower to any car, and that this one comes with 50 more, the increment is a bargain. There's lots of additional content, too—more safety gear, a higher-quality top, high and low beam HID headlights, a more powerful audio system, and better quality materials—so it's easy to see where the money was spent. And still, even at a somewhat higher price point, anything that can outrun it costs a lot more.

The Future

There's little question that the Viper will be a member of the Chrysler's lineup for a long, long time. In just a decade, it has garnered popularity among its owners and fans that matches that of the Mustang and Corvette—cars that have been building a legacy for 40 and 50 years respectively. It's the cornerstone of Chrysler's Performance Vehicle Operations group, and will still draw traffic to Dodge dealers. The previous platform lasted a decade, with one major revision and the introduction of an additional model about mid-way through its production life.

What's next? It's hard to say, and unfortunately, Dodge isn't telling. But there are a few conclusions we can draw. The upcoming Ram SRT-10 (see sidebar) is the first production model to share the Viper's powertrain, making good on the promise of that original 1994 concept, though doing so based on the new-for-2002 Ram platform. It's doubtful there are many other places or products where the big V-10 could be put to use (other than the handful of Tomahawk quadracycles Dodge has announced it will build), so this unique, 500-plus horsepower truck is probably the extent of additional platform sharing the Viper can offer.

Don't expect Viper development to stand still. The next logical step would be a new generation GTS Coupe. And we already know what it looks like; recall that the current Viper design showed up as the GTS-R concept car at the 2000 Detroit auto show. And of course the Viper Competition Coupe, the race version of the SRT-10, wears bodywork that looks like the slightly race-ified variant of the street GTS Coupe that is sure to follow sometime around the 2006 or 2007 model year. The previous generation GTS proved a strong seller its entire career, and the basic design work is complete, so this is all but a done deal as this book goes to print.

It's hard to imagine that the Viper will ever need any more power, but then again, 400 seemed like a world-beating number when the car was introduced. The V-10's power output has gone up a full 20 percent

This "ghosted" image shows the SRT-10s top in both up and down positions. Unlike the old "toupee and side curtains" arrangement, which was a time consuming mess to install or remove, the new convertible top drops in seconds (although the trunk must first be opened), and creates its own cover. *Wes Allison*

in the ensuing decade, yet companies like Mercedes-Benz AMG make luxury sport sedans putting out nearly that much. So perhaps there's room for 550? 600? Where it will end, no one is certain. Dodge may also elect to cook up a special edition Viper now and again, like the previous GT2 and ACR models.

Beyond that, it's possible that, after a long enough hiatus, the Viper will re-enter big bore sports car racing, another arena where the previous GTS-R racer proved literally a world-beater. But more than

one insider has told us that its not likely to happen until Dodge's stock car effort yields a NASCAR championship, so we'll have to wait and see.

No matter, the Dodge Viper enters its second decade with its popularity unabated, and its performance virtually unchallenged by anything that costs less than double its price. It will remain a uniquely American, hairy-chested muscle/sports car. The people who produce it, and the enthusiasts who buy it, wouldn't want it any other way.

SIX

Viper Variations

The amount of enthusiasm generated by the Viper is akin to dropping a very large rock in the middle of a pond: a significant ripple effect was bound to follow. Chrysler gained new understanding of the value of the "team approach" to designing and building cards. It also proved to the world, the car industry, and to *itself* that a large multinational corporation can develop products for niche markets. As discussed, Viper also drew an amazing amount of media reaction; Chrysler PR has probably lost count of how many magazine covers Vipers have appeared on over the years. It's only natural, then, to expect Viper's influence to extend to other Chrysler products,

Jet versus Snake might seem like an obvious win for the fighter plane, but it wasn't that easy. Dodge has staged two such match races at events benefiting the Luke Air Force Base Charity Fund. The first such endeavor in March 2002 pitted a Viper Competition Coupe against an F-16, with the jet narrowly nipping the Viper in the agreed-upon 1/2 mile distance; PVO's John Fernandez was at the wheel. The rematch, a year later, brought an F-16 up against a white, street legal SRT-10 driven by Herb Helbig. Herb was able to get a better launch, and he snaked the F-16 Fighting Falcon Viper for the win, evening the score. *DaimlerChrysler*

the aftermarket, car clubs, TV and movie types, and to the fertile imagination of the buying public. Viper engines have ended up in all sorts of interesting vehicles lately, including those built by Dodge, and others that could only come from the fertile imagination of the hot rodding public.

This is by no means a complete compendium on what people do to and with their Vipers, but it does indicate the sort of enthusiasm and creativity that surrounds and supports this phenomenal car.

Dodge Ram VTS Concept (1994)

Trucks are big business. In fact, the best-selling vehicle in America has been the Ford F-150 for many years running. And modified, personalized, downright *hot-rodded* trucks are a big part of the picture. So in 1994, with Dodge bringing out its first all-new pickup in more than 20 years—with the first-ever production V-10 engine—the Ram VTS concept vehicle is almost no surprise. The Ram's iron V-10 produces 300 horsepower and 450 ft-lb of torque, and it's no secret that it and the Viper's aluminum alloy "Copperhead" V-10 began life on nearby drawing boards. Dodge whipped up the VTS to have a little fun and to gain a little press. "We knew it would only be a matter of time until someone would try to pack a Viper V-10 engine into a Ram truck," said Chrysler designer Mike Castiglione at the Ram VTS's unveiling. "We thought Dodge ought to beat them to the punch."

The VTS carried the Viper V-10 and six-speed transmission, as well as prototype future Viper wheels. The special front air dam included Viper-style fog

The Ram VTS prototype carries as many Viper cues as would translate from roadster to pickup truck, including a special front fascia with fog lights and Viper GTS prototype wheels. The most important part was the V-10 underhood. Fortunately, Dodge didn't forget this idea, and it came back in the form of the Ram SRT-10 for 2003. *DaimlerChrysler*

Dodge turned heads when it fitted a Viper V-10 into a full-sized Ram truck, so why not try to cram one into a smaller pickup? The Dakota Sidewinder concept was one of Dodge's show toys at the November 1996 SEMA aftermarket show in Las Vegas, and it hinted at a few design cues that would appear on the new-for-1997 production Dakota. A 2,700-pound truck with 600 horsepower? Sounds like easy burnouts. *DaimlerChrysler*

lights, and the paint scheme matched the Viper GTS Coupe. It was built from a standard-cab Ram 1500 pickup.

Though the VTS drew both attention and admiration, Chrysler claimed it never intended to put the truck into production. This is understandable, given that others had tried marketing factory high-performance trucks and had experienced only moderate success. GMC's Syclone in 1991, with a turbo V-6, was dropped after two years in production; the Chevrolet SS 454 lived only a bit longer. Ford's Special Vehicle Team fared much better with its fine handling Lightning, but elected to drop it after the 1995 model year, though it returned in supercharged

form in 1999. The original VTS remained but a potent dream . . . for a while, anyway.

Skip Barber Driving School

Slightly modified sedans and detuned Formula Fords are common fare at many racing schools, but the Skip Barber curriculum includes Dodge Dakota V-8 pickups, Neons, open-wheel Dodge-powered Formula cars . . . and Vipers.

Barber opened his first racing school in 1975; as of 1995, all school cars were Dodge or Dodge-powered vehicles. This marketing arrangement is similar to that of the Bob Bondurant School of High Performance Driving, which uses GM products exclusively.

Viper Races Indy

Dodge was in a bind. It had wanted to promote its new Stealth and swung a deal with the Indianapolis Motor Speedway for the performance coupe to pace the 1991 500-mile race. One rub: the Stealth was built for Dodge by Mitsubishi, along with Mitsu's own quite similar 3000 model. When the word got out that what is essentially a Japanese car was scheduled to pace the Greatest Spectacle in Racing, a rumble of protest issued forth from American enthusiasts. The fix? How about the new-for-1992 Dodge Viper?

Another problem: Team Viper was not yet ready to build production cars, much less one that would be showcased in front of more than 20 million race fans. As usual, they rose to the challenge, hand-building an essentially production-spec Viper prototype capable of exceeding the Speedway's performance criteria—in less than three months' time.

More than 1,800 miles of testing proved the car race-day ready, and two cars were actually prepared for pace-car duty. On May 26, 1991, racing legend and Viper patriarch Carroll Shelby paced Rick Mears' victory in the 75th Anniversary Indianapolis 500. It was Rick's fourth win, and also a big win for Team Viper. What began as a marketing and PR nightmare turned into a dream ride for this most American machine.

Since the Viper's appearance at the 1991 500 proved such a successful part of the car's 1992 model year launch, Chrysler PR and marketing types went back to the same well for 1996. With the GTS Coupe on the way for 1997, it proved a logical move. Fortunately there was no such Stealth-related PR hurdle to climb; the GTS Coupe was clearly the right player from the very beginning.

This time around, Shelby's pal (and then Chrysler President) Bob Lutz was called on for pace car duties. It was a somewhat historic race since 1996 was also the first year of the new Indy Racing League (IRL). As many of the new series drivers had little or no experience at the Speedway, it was anticipated that the pace car would see a lot of action—which it did. It performed flawlessly, as did Buddy Lazier, earning his first Indy 500 victory that day.

"Follow me, guys!" Bob Lutz at the wheel of the Viper GTS prototype used to pace the 1996 edition of the Memorial Day Classic. As expected, no performance modifications were required. Pacing this race was historic because it marked the first year of the new Indy Racing League. *DaimlerChrysler*

Various Barber courses are offered on several tracks around the country.

The Viper plays an important role at the Dodge/Skip Barber Driving School and is used primarily for autocross portions of the course. It allows the driver a chance to learn in a seriously high-performance vehicle, yet, being a two-seater, an instructor can ride along to observe the student's technique, something not possible in a single seater. According to Rick Roso, the school's PR manager, the Vipers are "*very* popular" with students and teachers alike!

Viper Television Show

You need only look at the specially-equipped Aston Martin DB5 driven by James Bond in *Goldfinger* and *Thunderball* to understand the impact that a starring role in a major movie or TV show can have on a car's reputation . . . and sales. Remember Martin Milner's Corvette in *Route 66?* Sales of black and gold Pontiac Trans Ams skyrocketed after the success of Burt Reynolds' *Smokey and the Bandit*. And so on.

When NBC not only selected the Viper (and several other Chrysler vehicles) to appear in its 1994 action-adventure series, but actually named the show *Viper*, it seemed to be a dream marketing vehicle (pun intended) for Dodge. "In a future where criminals outgun and outrun the law, one man and one machine will change all the rules," according to NBC PR materials. The show starred James McCaffery as Michael Payton, a bad-guy-turned-good who now goes after his old gang, "The Outfit."

The Viper's bag of tricks made most other show-

Viper series star James McCaffery suits up to take a Viper cutaway camera car for a "ride." This rig is towed behind another vehicle for close-up moving shots; a big improvement over the old technique of a movie screen sitting behind the car. *Paramount Television and NBC*

The "Defender" Viper from the TV series *Viper*. Although the show was less than a hit, it was great fun to watch a standard red Viper roadster "morph" into this car. The series' sets and special effects were well done. Metalcrafters, which has built many of Chrysler's modern concept cars, designed the Defender.

time vehicles, such as the "KITT" Firebird from *Knight Rider*, look tame. In off-duty guise, it appeared to be a standard red Viper. When it was time for action the car "morphed" into the armored "Defender" Viper, a gray hardtop complete with "fangs" in the grille. An advanced satellite system, tractor beams, and the like were employed as plot devices intended to render the villains' cars helpless.

Several standard Vipers, plus the Defender show

Left: The Viper has claimed a number of celebrity owners, among them consummate car guy and *The Tonight Show* host Jay Leno and *Frasier* star Kelsey Grammer (who ultimately wrecked his). *David Newhardt*

Below: A Viper kit car? Unfortunately, someone had to try. A British firm named the Fiero Factory (which should tell you something) cobbled together this Viper almost-look-alike. The car could be built on a Corvette C4 chassis and powered by a Chevy engine, or upon its own chassis design employing the powertrain and suspension from a—believe it or not—Ford Granada. The overriding question about the entire project remains: why? *Fiero Factory*

2003 Dodge Viper SRT-10 Venom 650R

With only 500 horsepower and 525 ft-lb of torque on tap, a 2003 Dodge Viper SRT-10 just isn't fast enough for some people. To put added bite in the already ridiculously fast snake, aftermarket venom is available, including from long-time Viper tuners Hennessey Performance. Two years ago, some customers raised concerns about Hennessey's business practices (we heard from a few), and the jury is still out on the validity of those claims. But the distractions haven't stopped Hennessey from developing a cache of new speed parts. We tested two turnkey engine packages, the Venom 600 and Venom 650R, one of which notched the quickest quarter-mile time we've recorded on stock tires.

The Venom 600 package incorporates a host of traditional go-fast upgrades that focus primarily on moving air in and out in quicker fashion. A custom air-inlet tract uses twin free-flowing air filters that mate with a ported throttle body. CNC-ported cylinder heads increase intake port flow from 275 cfm to 325 and also raise the compression ratio from 9.6:1 to 10.2:1, thanks to head decking. A Comp Cams custom ground hydraulic roller camshaft sends opening and closing cues to valves upgraded with extreme-duty valve springs and titanium retainers. Special computer calibration still allows the fortified 8.3-liter V-10 to run on premium unleaded pump gas and comply with 50-state smog certification, according to Hennessey. Venom 1.8-inch-diameter stainless-steel 5-to-1 headers team with high-flow catalytic converters to quickly vent spent exhaust fumes and deliver a more throaty exhaust note. The $19,500 Venom 600 package includes professional installation, chassis dyno testing, road testing, and a limited two-year warranty, along with the requisite Venom 600 badging to impress your buddies.

Not enough? Consider the Venom 650R package that includes all the above hardware and takes it to the next level by way of a stroker short-block: The 522-cube 650R incorporates JE 10.8:1 forged pistons with heavy-duty pins, moly rings, longer than stock Manley Pro forged-steel connecting rods, and a custom-machined stroker crankshaft. A Comp Cams roller cam is employed along with an upgraded fuel system and specific computer programming to deliver a wider power-band with gobs more torque than stock. Independent chassis dyno testing of the Venom 650R verified 587 horsepower and 584 ft-lb of torque measured at the rear tires. That translates to about 675 horses at the flywheel, assuming an industry-standard 15-percent drivetrain loss.

On the highway, the Venom 650R remains docile during cruising—actually even mellower than a stock SRT-10; but at the track, the package is vicious. Running on stock Michelin run-flat 19-inch radials, we drove the Venom 650R to an amazing 10.76-second quarter mile—making this the quickest stock-tired vehicle we've tested. With cautious throttle modulation, we hustled the 650R to a 3.0-second 0-to-60-mph sprint that beats all-wheel-drive super-exotics like the Lamborghini Murciélago by over half a second. If there's a downside to this performance story, it'll be the hit to your pocketbook, as the 650R package will set you back a solid $34,500. We suggest skipping the Venom 650R badging; let your time slips do the bragging. – John Kiewicz, reprinted courtesy *Motor Trend*

Hazing the skins" is seldom a problem for any Viper, but this 675-horsepower Hennessey-modified SRT-10 makes it even easier, seen here on its way to another sub-11 second quarter-mile pass. *John Kiewicz*

	Viper SRT-10	Venom 650R
0-60 mph	4.0	3.0
1/4 mile	11.77@123.63	10.76@128.67
Braking, 60-0, ft	97	98
0-100-0 mph, sec	12.2	10.4

Collecting Viperabilia *by Maurice Q. Liang*

Whether you own a Viper or not, you can satisfy some of that Viper-lust by collecting Viper memorabilia, or Viperabilia. Viperabilia collecting began as soon as the first Viper concept appeared in 1989. The first Viper toy was Galoob's red Micromachines RT/10 concept car. Since they didn't have a license from Dodge, the toy was quickly pulled off the market, so there aren't a lot of them out there. Other than that, there was a factory issued plastic promotional model from Ertl/AMT, model kits from Ertl and Revell, some shirts and hats, and a couple of posters. That was it, at least at the beginning.

But once the car caught the attention of the public, toy manufacturers jumped on the Viper bandwagon. Soon, Viper models and die-casts were available in all scales, from tiny 1/144 cars that were barely an inch long, to 1/4 scale go-karts. Attesting to the popularity of Viper, Brian Hannah, product manager for Mattel's Hot Wheels Collector Series said, "Viper has been a perennial seller for us. There are also many unlicensed 'Viper-like' models."

Serious collectors not only want the different models, they often collect different colors and variations. The more rare, the better. For example, Matchbox made around 25 samples of the Viper RT/10 concept car for its salespeople to show customers. But when they didn't get the license from Dodge, they modified the mold and sold it as the Sunburner instead. Now those Viper concept models are very desirable. Matchbox also had plans to sell 1/64 and 1/32 models of the *Viper* TV show crime-fighting car, the Defender; it was even listed in their catalog. But when the TV show failed to catch on, they abandoned plans to produce the toys, so only a few prototypes exist.

Viperabilia comes in other forms, too—hats, shirts, underwear, jewelry, dishes —even solid chocolate Vipers. There's also special memorabilia available only at the Viper Owner's Invitationals. Each event generates its own unique set of collectibles, such as engraved wine bottles, coasters, and banners, as well as the highly-coveted table centerpieces. You have to be there to get this stuff, and most people hang on to it.

"Paper" is also collectible. From Viper ads and magazine articles, to Viper brochures, to the more sought after press kits handed out to journalists when each new model is introduced. If you're really extreme, you even collect things like store and dealer displays that feature a Viper on it.

With collecting Viperabilia, you have to be quick. If you see it, buy it, because it may not be around for long. Viper toys are usually the first to fly off the shelves. And if you think a Viper brochure is hard to obtain now, try finding one twenty-five years from now. Unless you have unlimited space and funds, it's a good idea to pick a Viper collecting theme that's more limited than "Anything Viper." Choose your favorite color combination or maybe a certain scale of models. Fortunately, with the Internet and eBay, it's easier than ever to collect now. Happy hunting.

Maurice Liang has been collecting Viperabilia since the concept car first appeared in 1989 and has amassed one of the most comprehensive collections of Viper memorabilia in the world. Liang owns a Viper GTS and an RT/10, and co-founded the Viper Club of America. He is currently authoring the Viper Buyer's Guide.

Maurice Q. Liang

car (styled by Neil Walling and crew as an official factory project), were employed in production. One had its entire front end removed to create a camera car, and at least two Vipers were fitted with 360-ci V-8 engines and automatic transmissions for stunt work. Though the show featured glossy sets and solid special effects work, the net result was a marginal effort at best. To quote one particular TV critic, it wasn't exactly *Masterpiece Theatre*. NBC canceled *Viper* after just 13 episodes. *Viper* reappeared in 1996 as a first-run syndicated series, this time making it through three full seasons before being permanently parked.

Vipers have also made several other TV and movie appearances. One of the most recent was the use of a yellow SRT-10 in 2003's street racing, car-chasing *2 Fast 2 Furious*. Though only one car appeared in the movie, a total of four were employed in the filming and stunt work. Other than a bit of paintwork to make the "Dodge" and "Viper" logos more visible, the cars were unmodified.

The Aftermarket

Former Chrysler President Bob Lutz said, "Power in the Viper is like your personal bank account.

Continued on page 90

Top and above: Besides factory projects like the original Viper-powered Ram and Sidewinder concepts, Viper V-10s have found themselves under all sorts of hoods. It looks like it absolutely grew under the hood of this 1969 Dodge Charger, and provides an interesting alternative to the period Hemi or 440 Six-Pack. Viper engines have powered numerous street rods, including a 1954 Plymouth custom called the Sniper. *Barrett-Jackson Auctions*

2004 Dodge Ram SRT-10

Now, *that's* a truck

It took Dodge a decade to fulfill the promise set forth by that original Ram VTS of 1994: a full-sized truck packing a Viper engine. But it appears that the Ram SRT-10 will have been worth the wait. The current Ram platform was new for the 2002 model year, and everyone agrees that the 500 horsepower cranked out by today's Viper V-10 is cooler than the "paltry" 400 of the original VTS concept. Why build a monster Ram now? Dodge's own press materials clarify the mission with a clear and succinct proclamation: "Because we can. The Dodge Ram SRT-10 mission is simple: biggest, baddest, and fastest."

The Ram SRT-10 is one of three very different products developed under what is now the PVO banner (the other two being the Viper itself, and the Neon-based Dodge SRT-4).

While, fundamentally, the Ram SRT-10 is a short bed, half-ton Ram with an engine transplant, it's considerably more than that: the PVO group worked hard to ensure that the truck has the suspension, brakes, aero touches, and look to match its 8.3-liter, 500-horse V-10. The rolling stock, for example, is positively huge: 22-inch alloy wheels with low profile, high performance tires. The four wheel disk brake system's rotors are an impressive 15-inches up front, and 14-inches in back. Bilstein provides the shocks, and unlike most trucks, the suspension was calibrated to maximize handling, not tow ratings or payload.

Relatively few tweaks were required to get the V-10/T56 6-speed trans combo ready for super truck duty. There are revised exhaust manifolds, a slightly-modified oil pan, new engine and transmission mounts, a Ram-specific air cleaner

exhaust system (with four Viper catalysts), and a very cool long-handled Hurst shifter. The Dana 60 rear axle runs 4.11 gears and a Hydra Lock limited slip diff. Another important suspension component is the traction bar system, designed to combat the combination of a vehicle that carries relatively little weight over its rear axle, and the tire-melting effects of 500 horsepower. One Dodge truck team member told us that during tests performed with slick tires, the Ram SRT-10 hooks up so well, and launches so hard, it will actually "wrinkle" the tire sidewalls, just like a real dragster.

A Ram is hardly the most aerodynamic device ever built, so considerable attention was paid to aerodynamics. A few lessons were borrowed from Dodge's own NASCAR Craftsman Truck series teams, and the SRT-10 spent time in the company wind tunnel. The front fascia is a unique piece, which incorporates an integrated front splitter to keep the nose stable—important for a truck with genuine 150 miles per hour capabil-

ity. There's also a rear wing which is fully functional and reduces lift. Inside, the SRT-10 gets heavily bolstered sport seats, carbon-fiber-look trim on the steering wheel, full instrumentation—even the Viper's red starter button. The color combinations, as of this writing, are the same as the Viper's too: red, black, and silver.

The Ram SRT-10 was just coming to market as this book was written, so it's difficult to predict how it will be received in the marketplace. But one Dodge dealer told us he's had a lot of interest in the maximum strength Ram from one particular group. You guessed it: current Viper owners.

A large, functional air intake, an aggressive lower fascia with fog lights, and that trademark cross-hairs grille visually tie the 2004 Dodge Ram SRT-10 to the sports car that gave it 500 horsepower. Installation of the DVX-series V-10 into the Ram was generally straightforward but still required considerable re-engineering of many details to make it production ready. The Ram cabin also enjoys several Viper cues. An optional automatic trans? As with the Viper, the answer is "don't even go there." *DaimlerChrysler*

Skip Barber instructor Walter Irvine and course participant Ashley Launey probe the limits of adhesion in one of the school's new SRT-10s. Barber also uses previous generation RT/10s and GTS Coupes at its various schools. *Rick Roso, courtesy Dodge/Skip Barber Driving School*

Dan Fitzgerald attempted to forge the "missing link" between Carroll Shelby's original Cobras and the Viper. Fitzgerald was one of Shelby's top-selling dealers back in the good old days, and he went on to develop a special-edition Shelby-ized Viper. *Visual Graphics*

There's no such thing as too much of it." No matter how much performance and style a manufacturer builds into an automobile, there is an imaginative aftermarket industry waiting to offer parts and accessories intended to increase one or both elements. The Viper is no different. It's natural for enthusiasts to personalize their machines, especially with an automobile that was at first offered in only one body style—and in only one color.

Viper owners' approach toward modification of their cars tends to take two distinctly different forms: (1) those wishing to add on a few goodies to accessorize their toy, or make it different from everyone else's, and (2) serious hot rodders for whom 400 to 500 horsepower still isn't enough. The most common choices for those in the first category are aftermarket wheels, lighting, intake and exhaust systems, interior upgrade trim, and replacement body panels. "Type As" in the second group generally go for more performance-oriented suspensions, brake kits, and big horsepower adders. Several aftermarket companies offer twin turbo kits, nitrous oxide injection, "stroker" blocks for more displacement, hot camshafts, and ported and polished intakes and cylinder heads; the sky, and the budget, are truly the limit. But 600 horsepower Vipers are not uncommon, and a few "hand grenades" have been built (primarily for magazine testing and bragging rights purposes) that crank out more than that.

The answer to a question nobody asked? Automotive sculpture? Ridable engine stand? Everyone has an opinion about the Dodge Tomahawk concept, er, vehicle, which made its debut at the 2003 Detroit auto show. Yes, that's a Viper V-10 sitting between where the driver/rider's knees sit. Amazing as it seems, Dodge announced it would hand-build ten of the "bikes" for its most ardent customers and collectors. The price? $555,000. At least one Tomahawk was to be sold through the Neiman Marcus holiday catalog. *DaimlerChrysler*

APPENDIX A

Additional Information

Viper Quarterly

Produced by the J. R. Thompson Company for the Dodge division of Chrysler Corporation.

VQ is not a book, but a high-quality owner's/ enthusiast's magazine published four times a year. It contains a high concentration of color art, interviews with PVO executives, engineers, and team members, light technical information, as well as lots of news, letters, and photos from Viper owners. Well worth subscribing to. Contact: *Viper Quarterly*, P.O. Box 2117, Farmington Hills, MI 48333. 800-998-1110. Visit www.viperclub.org or www.4adodge.com

Viper: Pure Performance by Dodge

From the editors of *Consumer Guide*. Published in 1993 by Publications International, Ltd., 7373 N. Cicero Ave. Lincolnwood, IL 60646.

This was the first book ever published solely on the Viper. It focused primarily on the early days of the car's development and debut in 1992. There are good archival photos of the prototypes, the first Viper assembly plant, comparisons with other big-inch sports cars, and details on the "team concept" then just spawning at Chrysler. Given when this volume was published, it should come as no surprise that virtually every production car shown is red; colors and the GTS were yet to come. Limited in scope, but handsome and worth having if the Viper's development and pre-launch days are your primary interest.

Dodge Viper on the Road

Compiled by R. M. Clarke. Published by Brooklands Books, Ltd., Surrey, England.

Books usually reflect on specific automobiles or entire marques from a historical perspective, but enthusiast magazines focus on cars as they come out, with an emphasis on road testing. This volume is a collection of reprint articles and road tests from most well-known buff magazines: *Road & Track, Car and Driver, Motor Trend,* and the like. The pages are all black and white, and being reprints, the graphics are only fair. But the information is solid, and it's fun to compare the road-test performance results. Still in print as of this writing, and a lot of info for the money.

Dodge Viper

By Dan Carney

This 168-page hardcover book does a comprehensive job of chronicling the Viper's history and development up to and including the launch of the SRT-10. Carney is a technically savvy author, so there's plenty of "nuts and guts" information, plus a nice display of color and black-and-white photography. The walk through the assembly plant makes a nice chapter, and there's plenty of primary interview material. There are a few errors and occasional questions of balance, but overall, well worth having. $34.95 as of this writing, available from MBI Publishing Company, 800-826-6600.

Viper Club of America

Enthusiast clubs just make owning special cars easier, and a lot more fun. "Enthusiasm and people" is what the Viper Club of America is all about, according to its first president, Maurice Liang. As of this writing, there are more than three-dozen regional VCOA clubs around the country. They generally feature local events, a club newsletter, information exchange, social gatherings, and the like. The club, which is fully support by DaimlerChrysler, puts on fabulous

annual (or nearly annual) "Owners Invitational" conventions. Don't own a Viper without a VCOA membership. For information contact: Viper Club of America, c/o J. R. Thompson Company, PO Box 2117, Farmington Hills, MI 48333. 800-998-1110. Visit www.viperclub.org, or www.4adodge.com

The Viper Faithful gather in Long Beach for another Viper Owners Invitational. Two factory Competition Coupes are seen foreground. *David Newhardt*

APPENDIX B

Production and Evolution

Viper Production Numbers

1992: 282	1999: 1248
1993: 1403	2000: 1789
1994: 3086	2001: 1751
1995: 1577	2002: 1667
1996: 710	2003: 1873 (through August 2003)
1997: 1788	Source: DaimlerChrysler
1998: 1216	Public Relations

SUMMARY OF MAJOR PRODUCT CHANGES 1992-2002

1992 Model Year
Original-specifications roadster; Red exterior only available color
No air conditioning

1993 Model Year
Reverse lock-out feature added to transmission

Windshield antenna replaced most antennas
Battery relocated to left frame rail
Front and rear bumpers now of composite material

1994 Model Year
Black and tan interior color scheme added
Factory-installed air conditioning available
Passenger-door grab handle added

1995 Model Year
New one-piece cast intake manifold

1996 Model Year
RT/10
Higher output V-10; 415 horsepower
All-aluminum front and rear suspension
Rear-exit exhausts replace sidepipes
New wheel designs
Factory-offered removable fiberglass hardtop replaces previous cloth-and-frame top
GTS
GTS coupe model introduced mid-year featuring side glass windows
Revised, lighter weight V-10; new block, heads, cooling tract; 450 horsepower

1997 Model Year
RT/10
Roadster bodystyle received 450-horsepower GTS engine
Revised interior incorporates driver/passenger side air bags, power side glass windows
Removable fiberglass hardtop replaces previous cloth-and-frame top
GTS
Yellow wheel package
Red exterior

1998 Model Year
Both models
Next-generation driver side airbags
Passenger side air bag on/off switch
Revised exterior colors
Limited edition "GT2" model commemorating 1997 FIA GT2 championship; white with blue trim, 100 built.

1999 Model Year
Both models
New 18-inch aluminum wheels with Viper-specific Michelin Pilot Sport tires
Optional Connolly leather trimmed interior
ACR (American Club Racer) Group model homologated for club racing (Spring 1999 intro, available on GTS coupe only)

2000 Model Year
Both models
Child seat tether anchorage
GTS
Revised ACR Group model featuring high performance oil pan, Dynamic Suspensions adjustable shock absorbers, revised ACR badging

2001 Model Year
Both models
Standard anti-lock brakes

2002 Model Year
Both models carry over unchanged
GTS Final Edition, last 360 Viper GTS coupes built, red with white stripes, special badging

Source: *Chrysler*

INDEX

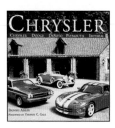
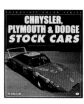

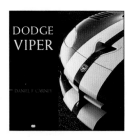
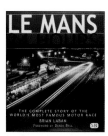